Doing Things Right
in Matters of the Heart

D0786183

Doing Things Right
in Matters of the Heart

John Ensor

CROSSWAY BOOKS

A PUBLISHING MINISTRY OF
GOOD NEWS PUBLISHERS
WHEATON, ILLINOIS

Library of Congress Cataloging-in-Publication Data
Ensor, John M.
 Doing Things Right in Matters of the Heart / John Ensor.
  p. cm.
 Includes bibliographical references and index.
 ISBN 13: 978-1-58134-842-2 (tpb)
 ISBN 10: 1-58134-842-8
 1. Sex role—Religious aspects—Christianity. I. Title.
BT708.E57   2007
261.8'357—dc22   2006037264

CH		17	16	15	14	13	12	11	10	09	08	07
15	14	13	12	11	10	9	8	7	6	5	4	3	2	1

To my Kristen,
with love.
Your John E.

Contents

Section One

Matters of the Heart

Chapter One

Introductory Matters in Matters of the Heart

I am not so nice,
To change true rules for odd inventions.

SHAKESPEARE

The simple believes everything,
but the prudent gives thought to his steps.

PROVERBS 14:15

*B*ecause I wanted it badly, I did not think clearly. I was bent on having it, so I was foolish in the way I pursued it. I so hoped it was true that I fell for what was false. I heard only what I wanted to hear and looked right past the red flags. I did not handle things wisely; I was clueless but did not know it (which means I was profoundly clueless). At the time, it seemed so good. How did it turn out so badly? When it all played out, I was right back where I started, only poorer, embarrassed, and embittered. I felt used, and I felt stupid, mainly because I was used, and I was stupid.

I'm talking about a used car and the way I went about obtaining it. I went online and was defrauded out of four thousand dollars. Looking back, it was all there on the web site—general guidelines on doing things right when purchasing a used car online. There was a special section about online fraud. I suppose I never considered that I'd be a victim of fraud, so I never noticed the link or read it before venturing on.

The webmaster knew I needed instruction. He knew something about human nature—about what Abe Lincoln would call "the lower angels of our nature," about people at their predatory worst who feed on people in their most gullible innocence and ignorance. So there it was, spelled out and illustrated. Here is what to look for and what to avoid—sure signs of fraud and other straightforward instructions and guidelines for doing things right when buying a used car online. As the webmaster, after all, he wants his clients to find what they are looking for and to obtain it in a way that leaves all parties involved pleased. But I did not consult the webmaster.

There Is a Way That Seems Right

The Proverbs warn us: "The simple believes everything, but the prudent gives thought to his steps" (14:15). I *know* this is true. Another proverb says, "There is a way that *seems* right to a man, but its end is the way to death" (14:12). I think this refers to the common practice of following our own judgment without informing it with the wisdom of others or instructing it with a sense of right and wrong, wise and foolish. It is the error of self-confidence asserting itself with no foundation other than its having originated from self.

It is one thing to act foolishly—to be a simpleton—when buying a used car. It is another when it comes to matters of the heart. The stakes are infinitely higher. Failure here means weeping into tear-stained pillows through sleepless nights. It means hot flashes of shame. It means spiritual incapacitation when it comes to things like prayer and worship. It can mean single-parenting or child support. It has dragged too many off to Planned Parenthood with an innocent in the womb, where the Proverb finds literal fulfillment: "There is a way that seems right . . . but its end is the way to death" (Proverbs 14:12). Should we escape this ultimate consequence, we are still awash with self-doubt and self-loathing. We are spent and left poorer in spirit and zest for life. We are less trusting and have less to work with when we finally muster the courage to try again. We identify with more country music and blues than is good for anyone's well-being.

This book is about doing things *right* in matters of the *heart*. It is for those who know by painful experience, if not by observation, that the postmodern paradigm of meeting up, hooking up, shacking up, and breaking up is bankrupting the rich treasure of love itself. It doesn't matter that this is what most people are doing. You can see it does not ring true. It does not work. It is time to revolt against the times, to consult the webmaster, to learn how to spot fraud in matters of the heart, and to enter into a relationship as one "who gives *thought* to his steps" (Proverbs 14:15). To that end, I want to speak plainly and directly about right and wrong, wise and foolish, even good and evil, that you may avoid being defrauded and find what you want in matters of the heart.

Borrowing My Learning Curve

My oldest son called me about the car. He was remarkably polite and restrained when I told him the news. If ever there was a moment for ridicule, this was it. "Pop, you dope! How could you be that dumb?" I think he was a bit shocked. He went online and reviewed all my steps, tracing out the error of my ways. He was consoling. He was also borrowing my learning curve!

It is not the first time. He got married at age twenty-four, young by the measure of our times. His wife, Alisha, was even younger, only twenty-one. In open affront to our materialistic values, they got married while they were both still in college, with some twenty-thousand dollars in school debt hanging over their heads. They did not live together prior to marriage, and contrary to almost every "boy meets girl" movie made in Hollywood during the last twenty years, they chose to be abstinent until they were wed.

They did not wait to finish school but they did wait to be sexually intimate. Surely this is all wrong! I hope to persuade you that it was all very right. My wife and I did the same thing. We met. We melted. We refrained and abstained. We thought (mostly *I* thought) about our future. I wrestled with the M-word. I argued with myself: "I can't really be in love, can I? Why can't I picture my life without her? I only met her a month ago! I'm still in college and the most expensive thing I own is my forty-five-dollar tennis racket. I drive a car with a missing fender! How can I even think about m . . . ma . . . mar . . . marriage?"

Martin Luther once received a letter from a young man in love and struggling with the M-word. Luther wrote back, "Stop thinking about it and go to it right merrily."[1] This is what I decided to do. Only, unlike my son, I was only twenty-two-years-old.

Then again, maybe my son did not learn this pattern from his parents, but from his grandparents, who first met as babies in their church nursery. They were high school sweethearts; indeed neither had ever had another date. They wanted to be together. In those days, there was a clear cultural expectation of waiting till marriage before practicing intimacy. So they married—at age nineteen. Should their good health continue, my wife's parents will celebrate their sixty-fifth wedding anniversary just as this book goes to press.

The Purpose of This Book

The objective of this book is to provide a winsomely radical alternative to the prevailing ideas, almost absolute doctrines, that guide our current thinking about manhood and womanhood and define our actions and expectations when pursuing matters of the heart. It is not my aim to be radical for radical's sake. Paradoxically, it is

---

[1] Martin Luther, *Letters of Spiritual Counsel, Vol. 18*, Library of Christian Classics (London: SCM Press LTD, 1945), 274.

radical only in that postmodernity has radically gone and changed all the rules and definitions, and I say with Shakespeare, "I am not so nice, to change true rules for odd inventions." [2]

This book presupposes that you too question the status quo and have enough independence of thought and willpower to wonder if previous generations, though blind to some faults, might have some wisdom and insight for you, to which the current age has shut their eyes and stuck their fingers in their ears in a rush to create new truth at every turn.

If you are ready to give thought to your steps and can muster the courage to be a nonconformist, this book will give you much to consider and lots of decisions to make. "Every mind is a mason," wrote Victor Hugo (1802–1885).[3] The purpose of this book is to provide you stone with which you can fashion a strong, enduring, and satisfying plan for doing things right in this most tender and precious matter of the heart.

Mr. Wonderful

A while back, a staff member introduced her husband to me. "John, I want you to meet my husband, *Mr. Wonderful*."

I smiled. Such high praise can be the stuff of high irony. I looked at him to read his reaction. "Mr. *Wonderful*?" I said, needling him as I reach out to shake his hand. "That's a lot to live up too."

He blushed, but she went on. "No, I mean it. He is such a wonderful husband to me. I can't help but say it."

Then she rattled off a few of the things he did to make her so fulfilled and happy. I was in awe. Here was a woman simply enjoying the love of a good man and saying it as if it were as normal as iced tea in August. It sounded radical—*winsomely* radical.

Her delight in him and in their marriage was a stark reminder to me that no matter how many cynics speak of the war between the

---

[2]Shakespeare, *The Taming of the Shrew*, 3.1.80.
[3]Victor Hugo, *The Hunchback of Notre Dame* (New York: Barnes and Noble, 2004, orig. 1831), 244.

sexes, no matter how many times we hear that half of all marriages
end in divorce, no matter how many diatribes are written by angry
feminists, and no matter how many beer commercials present men
and women at their worst stereotypical selves, there are examples
of mature manhood and womanhood all around us. They are in our
churches. They are in our extended families. They are in the neigh-
borhood. They are people, full of human frailty to be sure, who
have nonetheless, learned to do things right in matters of the heart.
As a result, they are reaping the wonderful benefits of a healthy,
enduring, mutually satisfying love affair with one another.

The Pudding Test

Wouldn't you like to sit down with a man whose wife calls him
"Mr. Wonderful" and ask him about doing things right in matters of the heart? He is the one with true authority to write about
matters of the heart. His wife's joy is the proof of his pudding.
Tragically, soon after this greeting, my coworker's husband was
diagnosed with cancer. He has since died. So you are stuck with
my insights. But I have pudding too.

My situation is similar to that of the preacher C. J. Mahaney.
In his book *Humility: True Greatness*, he wrote, "I'm a proud man
pursuing humility by the grace of God."[4] We would be suspicious
if he claimed true greatness as an authority on humility.

In the same vein, I write about love and marriage and need
to admit that my own wife does not go around calling me "Mr.
Wonderful." But it will do no good to write about doing things right
in matters of the heart without having some of my own pudding by
which to prove it. The stakes are too high to write theoretically and
dispassionately in a "do as I say, not as I do" sort of way.

Dr. Expert

Wayne and Tamara Mitchell, who write a national weekly relationship advice column, ask a good question: "Why doesn't selling

---

[4]C. J. Mahaney, *Humility: True Greatness* (Sisters, OR: Multnomah, 2005), 13.

advice come out of getting it right? Why doesn't getting it right precede selling it?"[5] Their critique is aimed at relationship gurus John Gray and Barbara De Angelis.

John is the author of the best-selling book *Men Are from Mars, Women Are from Venus*. He was married to the best-selling author Barbara De Angelis, author of *How to Make Love All the Time* and *Secrets about Men Every Woman Should Know*. Along the trail of their lucrative lecture tour and book sales, John and Barbara divorced. Though their marriage ended, the lectures and advice continued. That's why the Mitchells warn readers about looking to experts, as defined by academic degrees and titles, rather than by the pudding of a life lived out together.[6] This is sound counsel.

In contrast, I remember as a young married man learning of the stunning decision of Dr. James Dobson of Focus on the Family. Author of some very popular books on marriage and child-raising, he was in high demand on the lecture circuit. Suddenly Dobson announced that he would no longer accept speaking invitations (with the rarest of exceptions). Why? Dobson was married and had young children. He did not want to write and speak expertly about matters of the heart while things fell apart at home. He wanted to do things right in matters of the heart. He wanted the authenticating proof of his counsel regarding male and female, marriage, and the high calling of parenthood to be written large in his real and everyday life. He wanted his own tasty pudding.

The Wisest Thing I've Ever Done

So what about me? I will tell my story along the way, for better and worse. For now it is important for you to know that my wife and I have enjoyed nearly thirty years together (and no, we have not been married for forty years!). We have remained true to each other and raised three children together. We have lived and are liv-

---

[5]Editorial comment posted at http://www.wayneandtamara.com/barbaradeangelis.htm.
[6]Tragically, Barbara is on marriage number five, yet she is now a co-editor of *Chicken Soup for the Couple's Soul*.

ing out the contents of this book. We believe it and we practice it. That we live it out imperfectly is evident to all who know us; what they do not know is how much better things are because we live it out to the degree that we do. I shudder to think where my life and marriage would be today if others had not passed on to me and my wife this compelling vision of manhood and womanhood and talked plainly about doing things right in matters of the heart. That they did and that we listened is the very outworking of God's grace in our lives.

As for real expertise, a banker, a teacher, a postman, or a receptionist you know might have as much as I, even more. I would highly recommend befriending real folks who have what you want. As for my authority, I point not to my degrees and licenses (which I have) but to the Bible. I will admit to being foolish for not consulting the webmaster when buying a used car. But I will declare it the wisest thing I have ever done to consult the Maker and Master of hearts when it comes to matters of the heart.

The Heart Knows Its Own Bitterness

As for my insight, much of it has been painfully forged from twenty-five years of pastoral counseling. "The heart knows its own bitterness" (Proverbs 14:10). I have heard my fair share of people pouring out their anguish. For twelve years I served as a pastor. For the last fifteen years I have preached and stirred up Christian communities to establish pregnancy help centers in and around Boston. Into these centers stream those bearing the bitter fruit of postmodern sexual ethics.

I have sat with hundreds of women and couples struggling with the fears and fallout of an unexpected pregnancy. In this context I've also seen the harm of sexually transmitted infections, the anguish of abortion, and the challenges of single parenting and adoption. I have seen the anorexic and the self-mutilating high achievers. I have talked to women who are ashamed of the sexual choices and angry at the bill of goods sold to them in the name of feminism. I have talked to teens who, unfortunately, listened atten-tively in their sex education classes and now in their twenties, sit astonished in the discovery that there is no condom for the heart!

They were taught that there is no right and wrong in such matters. Wrong! They were taught, "no one can tell you when you are ready." Why not? What are parents for? Where do ethics and morality come in to it? "Truth is what you make it for you person-ally," they were told. Now they know this is not true! Pregnancy is not a truth, subject to private interpretation. These educators undermined parental authority and moral and religious education and taught, "When you *feel* you are ready to have sex, it is *right* to have sex." Wrong again. The truth is that there is a way that *feels right* but leads to bitterness and death.

These anguished young women assume the fault lies with them. They must have missed something, so they try the whole routine of meeting up, hooking up, and breaking up—again and again. Five to ten years later they begin to realize it wasn't their execution that was at fault; the whole paradigm is false.

Young men wonder why abortion is not a safe, simple proce-dure, since everyone told them it was. "What's her hang up? Jus' git 'er done!" Or they stare at the baby waving a tiny hand on the ultrasound screen and wonder, "What does it mean for me to be a man *now*?" Before, it meant being good at seducing girls. Now, an impulse to run wages war against an impulse to do whatever it takes to protect this little innocent, pulsating with life and waving at him from within the mother.

Paralysis in Matters of the Heart

In contrast to the many young adults who are experiencing pain from doing things wrong are those young adults in paralysis, unsure of the right thing to do when it comes to matters of the heart.

I led a retreat for college students a few years ago. For the most part these were highly intelligent young adults from some of the forty-five colleges in the Boston area. They were either Christians or people actively considering the Christian faith. They were optimistic about their education and knew they had a bright future in terms of their career options. Something alarming happened there.

In group discussions with the men, they expressed confusion about role expectations and hesitation about doing *anything* in matters of the heart. I was thinking, "This cannot be good for the ladies!" After all, these are good guys! These are men who have a heart for God, a moral center, and so much more. These are the rainbow trout of our species. If women can't fish here, they are in trouble. All the other ponds are full of carp!

In my various conversations with the young women, they expressed that what they really wanted in a relationship was not what they were being taught by our popular culture that they were *supposed* to want. They wanted men to be, well, more *manly*! I was thinking, "Do the guys I just talked to know this?"

The young men, not being ready to act the way they are supposed to act these days, lacked confidence to act the way they really or naturally wanted to act. All was confusion, paralysis, and misunderstanding. Proverbs 13:12 says, "Hope deferred makes the heart sick, but a desire fulfilled is a tree of life." Is there not a life-fulfilling answer to this heart-wrenching paralysis?

Mason Work for the Soul

I think there is an answer. There is much that can be said about doing things right in matters of the heart. Others have tried to answer it more academically and more exhaustively.[7] This book is a user-friendly, basic version. In this section, I attempt to get to the heart of manhood and womanhood according to the Bible. What does it mean to be a *man* and not a woman? What is distinctively meaningful about being a *woman* and not a man? What marks

---

[7]See John Piper and Wayne Grudem, *Recovering Biblical Manhood and Womanhood* (Wheaton, IL: Crossway Books, 2006, orig. 1991). See also The Counsel on Biblical Manhood and Womanhood at www.cbmw.org.

the mature man? What does it mean to be, dare I say, a *godly* man? What marks the mature and godly woman and makes her attractive and fulfilled? How do we complement and fit together? In Section 2, I present direct and clear lines of approach. When a man loves a woman, and loves her well, what does that look like? Let us have an illustration! When a woman longs for Mr. Right, how should she conduct her search and lay the foundation for a healthy marriage?

I present a compelling vision of complementarity between the sexes. I propose action, but it is a complementary action for each. I bring into sharp relief the points of decision that will determine whether a person is undermining his or her own happiness or cementing in place another firm stone in a foundation of a lasting love and an enduring friendship. For, in the words of Ella Wheeler Wilcox:

> Love, to endure life's sorrow and earth's woe,
> Needs friendship's solid mason work below.

It is not chicken soup. It is mason work for the soul's happiness on earth.

Chapter Two

What the Heart Wants

I know how it feels to have wings on your heels,
And to fly down the street in a trance.
You fly down a street on the chance that you meet,
And you meet—not really by chance.

"HELLO, YOUNG LOVERS"
RICHARD RODGERS & OSCAR HAMMERSTEIN II

I adjure you, O daughters of Jerusalem,
If you find my beloved,
That you tell him
I am sick with love.

SONG OF SOLOMON 5:8

Not everybody wants to do things right in matters of the heart. Some simply want to do what they want to do, right or wrong.

Zsa Zsa's Zingers

Zsa Zsa Gabor, (1917–) has been called "the first celebrity to be famous solely for her celebrity."[1] She was Hollywood's glamour girl of the sixties, the Paris Hilton of her time.[2] Originally from Budapest, Hungary, she is famous for addressing everyone with her lovely accented "dahling." She made a career out of zinging love, romance, marriage, fidelity, and the mason work required of an enduring love. Though officially an actress, Zsa Zsa's legacy will always be her witty pokes at men and marriage:

- "A man in love is incomplete until he has married. Then he's finished."
- "I am a marvelous housekeeper. Every time I leave a man I keep his house."
- "I never hated a man enough to give him diamonds back."
- "I want a man who is kind and understanding. Is that too much to ask of a millionaire?"
- "Dahling, when you ask how many husbands I've had, do you mean apart from my own?"[3]

She did well with this *shtick* career wise. As a lifestyle, though, the price was high. Gabor was married nine times.

Baseball Kismet

Zsa Zsa's use of men was the perfect foil for Hugh Hefner and his emerging playboy philosophy of the same period. Hugh could not have succeeded, however, without the parallel emergence of the feminist movement. As women were taught to throw off modesty as a weakness, to be sexually aggressive, Hugh said, "Come to my house." The associative link continues today, as evidenced in the mainstreaming of pornography and so called soft-porn that is the staple of music videos. That this is the fruit of feminism is evident in that women see their sexual aggressiveness as part of their liberation, rather than as something they learned from *Playboy*. You

[1] See www.nndb.com/people/530/000025455/.
[2] Zsa Zsa Gabor was married to Conrad Hilton and is Paris Hilton's great aunt.
[3] Quoted from Murray Garrett, *Hollywood Moments* (New York: Abram Books), 26.

were once considered a cad if you saw women as so many bottles of wine to be tasted. Now you are a prude if you have a problem with recreational sex.

How truly radical this was, how odd the new invention, struck me again in reading *Cinderella Man*. In the 1930s, Max Baer was boxing's heavyweight champion of the world. Jeremy Schaap writes, "In a sports landscape lacking international basketball stars, soccer stars, and Formula One race-car drivers, the heavyweight champion wasn't just the best-paid or the most significant athlete in the world; he was—with possible exception of a few world leaders, such as Stalin or King George V—the most famous person on the planet."[4] Baer relished his fame and the female attention it brought him. I was stunned to read, however, that not just once, but *twice*, Baer was sued for "breach of promise" by women who shared his bed.[5] Breach of promise? How quaint. Obviously this tort died a victim of the sexual liberation.

Hip-hop music and magazines like *Glamour, Vogue,* and *Cosmopolitan* now assume that sex is the heart of the matter, rather than the *heart* being the heart of the matter. Trailing behind in their wake are "chick" movies. With rare exception they explain the dating game as first love, then sex, and perhaps marriage. If either a man or woman was dating someone else when *kismet* hit, they were, of course, sleeping with that other person. The plot line of chick movies follows the decoupling in order to follow kismet. The presupposition of these films—and by extension, the worldview of the writers—is that this is *how* it is done; this is the way everyone finds love. The key is to keep repeating the bonding and tearing process till you get a hit. Sort of like baseball really, only with kismet.

In the real world, however, most people want something very different in life. Get outside the morality-free and godless life of pop music and film, and you will find that when it comes to matters of the heart, the less-is-more theory is still very much alive. We

---

[4]Jeremy Schaap, *Cinderella Man* (Boston: Houghton Mifflin, 2005), xi.
[5]Ibid., 182.

are not *all* for picking up men or women like napkins, using them and tossing them aside. We want something deeper and richer—a healthy, tender, passionate, enduring, mutually fulfilling life with one good man or woman.

Am I Asking Too Much?

Greg Speck, a youth specialist, received this letter from a young teenaged girl. Listen to the real desire of her heart:

> I met this guy at a roller skating rink. We were too young to date, but I would see him once a week at the rink. After a month he invited me to his house. . . . His parents were gone, and he wanted to have sex with me. I really wanted to say no, but I was afraid of losing him, so I said yes. A week later we started to fight, and he broke up.
>
> I feel so crushed! The love turned to lust, and the lust to nothing. I feel so empty inside. I want a guy that will love me the person, not the body. I want someone I can love and someone to respect me. Am I asking too much?"[6]

She was young and innocent. She was naïve and very foolish. She was wrong about the right way to develop a relationship. But her heart's desire wasn't wrong.

Test All Things, Hold On to What Is True

A friend of ours had essentially the same story, though she was well educated, highly professional, and in her forties. The roller rink in this case was a restaurant. The protective role of parents was replaced by her internalized value system. The problem was that she didn't really trust herself any more than the young teen trusted that her parents knew what was best for her.

After an evening out together, our friend ended up at his apart-

[6]Greg Speck, *Sex: It's Worth Waiting For* (Chicago: Moody Press, 1989), 75.

ment. He led her towards the bedroom. She said no that night and for a month or so. He continued implying and promising devotion and kept moving her towards the bed.

My wife and I cautioned her that the man to whom she should want to say yes with fearless sexual abandon is a man who would not ask for it *at this point* in their relationship. "Test all things; hold on to what is true," we advised. The problem was that she did not want to test him and find him wanting. She simply *wanted* him.

She rationalized, "We are going to get married soon anyway. He said so himself!" Having yielded once, what was the point of stopping? Soon, however, the overall health of the relationship took a turn for the worse. He started expressing doubts about marriage. She started panicking and pushing. He pulled back further, and she was left, once again, drinking the bitter cocktail of nag and victim. He ended the relationship, politely, of course, and with all due concern about how much he cared for her and then said goodbye. He was on to the next challenge. Batter up!

Our friend had the same desire as the young teen along with the same fuzzy thinking about how to fulfill it. It contained no straining elements. It presented few qualifying hurdles. It was important to our friend that her man be a Christian. He soon claimed to be one; check that off. It was probably appealing that he was also a well-trained professional; he would be a good provider. Beyond that, however, her plan provided no protection. (Where is that condom for the heart?) The finish line was more of a general direction than a solid painted mark. (Where is that "breach of promise" provision?) Still, what she was striving for was clear and honorable; she wanted a life partner and a relationship that was healthy, tender, passionate, enduring, and mutually satisfying. Great goal, bad methodology.

Searching Eyes and Hungry Hearts

Even when we don't see this goal as what we want, it is still the driving force within. I stumbled upon this one day when four twenty-something women, good friends, arrived at the pregnancy center. Two of them needed a pregnancy test. They chatted together, trying not to be nervous, while the other two tried to be supportive.

"Where are those rascally men in your life?" I asked whimsically.

The eyes went up and around. Smirks and nods were duly given and received. The hurt, the sense of abandonment, the disgust, came pouring out. It was all so confusing to them. They weren't victims; they were coconspirators in their own destruction. They had learned from the culture how to dress and talk and put out. But it was supposed to lead somewhere other than to my pregnancy center, wasn't it?

When all fell silent, I rolled my chair over to them and asked, "How would you like me to tell you how to form a healthy, tender, passionate, enduring, mutually satisfying relationship with a man?"

They looked up with searching eyes and hungry hearts. They could not express what exactly they were looking for in all the flurry of their actions. They had read *Glamour* and the rest of that glop. They had been dressing up, going out, luring male attention, and controlling the situation according to all the tips and techniques suggested from those sage literary sources. It seemed to work at first, and then it proved hard and soon impossible to control. At some point they lost sight of what it was they wanted and began thinking only about what they should settle for.

When I painted the target as a healthy, tender, passionate, enduring, mutually satisfying friendship with a man, I laid their heart's desire bare. It is what most women want. "The secret longing of every woman's heart is to be wooed and won," writes Paula Rhinehart.[7] For the sake of clarity, I would add only "by a good and honorable man."

The idea of a prince charming is deep in the female heart. The

---

[7]Paula Rhinehart, *Sex and the Soul of a Woman* (Grand Rapids, MI: Zondervan, 2004), 73.

knight in shining armor and all things chivalrous remains a burning, pleasurable metaphor for what the heart wants. Like a coal, it may smolder under a heap of cold ash, the spent remnants of many reckless decisions regarding matters of the heart. But it burns nonetheless.

A Self-test for Women

Wendy Shalit, in her book, *A Return to Modesty*, provides an authenticating self-test for women regarding this matter of what the heart *truly* wants. She writes:

> It is always hard to separate what you really want from what you're supposed to want, but try is as a thought experiment. Women, when no one else is around, do you secretly long for a whole series of men; to arbitrarily marry one of them and then maybe have affairs, maybe not—to be cool and wait and see if anyone better comes along, and then divorce— or do you long for one enduring love? That's a loaded question, but still, if you could be guaranteed that no one would laugh at you, would it be the latter? If yes, why do you allow your culture to shatter your hopes? Why is it that you feel so dictated to, when you were supposed to be, above all, independent?[8]

There is no doubt that young women are being taught today to be sexually aggressive and to expect many partners. Modesty and restraint are considered signs of obsequious surrender to a foregone age of sexual repression. The strong woman is one who takes responsibility for her own body and who is smart enough to know how to use it. If she is good at it, it is assumed that she will have many partners. Women can and do get to this point. But this is *not* what they are by nature. This was not their starting point, only their settling point. Blow away the ash, and the ember yet burns for a healthy, tender, passionate, enduring, mutually satisfying relationship with just *one* man.

---

[8]Wendy Shalit, *A Return to Modesty* (New York: Touchstone Books, 1999), 93.

Am I Having Fun Yet?

Do men also have such a relationship as their heart's desire? They do. They absolutely do. In fact, I will go further. Men *need* this kind of relationship; and still further, they need it more than women do.[9] Yet to see this requires coming at it from a different angle. Let's begin at a point of common ground. Like women, men must distinguish between what they truly want and what they are expected to want or tempted to want. Let me illustrate.

When I was in high school, I remember going to a party with some friends. Everyone was shouting over the music, joking, and passing around cheap beer and jugs of even-cheaper wine. It was foul stuff, so I guzzled it fast and asked for more. I drank up, passed out, woke up, and threw up. I remember asking myself, "Am I having fun yet?" That was the first and last time I ever got drunk.

I was supposed to like partying. I certainly told my friends, "What a great party!" In truth, I hated it. So why say it was a great time? Because I was talking to my *friends* and having friends in high school is important when you are insecure and clueless as to who you are or what your life is about. As these were the only friends I had at the time, keeping them meant liking things that I did not like.

I have no doubt that I could have grown to like drunkenness with time and practice. But this is only to admit that I am a sinful man. Given the fact that my father was an alcoholic, I can probably assume that I might be genetically predisposed to alcoholism. Drinking, though, even to excess, would not tell me much about my heart's desire as a man. It would mask it. Had I followed this course, and if I had survived and found myself some thirty years later in recovery, some counselor would be helping me rediscover that what I really wanted in life were buddies, not Budweiser. Somehow they got cross-wired. In my long and painful road

---

[9] A fascinating read that evaluates the socializing power of marriage on manhood is George Gilder's book, *Men and Marriage* (Gretna, LA: Pelican, 1989). As a sociologist, he argues that marriage is actually a life-giving power to men. It reforms and directs their energies, gives meaning and purpose to their lives (which is why they become depressed or even violent during a breakup), and extends their mental health and longevity.

toward sobriety, I would have had to rediscover my taste for better things, the things I was designed to enjoy.

Making a Man Out of You

In the same way, our sinful nature and our sinful culture conspire to affirm the "boys will be boys" attitude. In some cases a young man's introduction to manhood is seen in teaching him to bed women. His "first time" is the initiation rite. One brother in my church told me how on his sixteenth birthday his father took him to a prostitute "to make a man out of me." He told this to me with great disgust for his father. I do not remember if he told me he was for it or afraid of it at the time. He was probably both afraid and curious. What we can be certain about is that he was for winning his father's approval. That was the need and desire of his heart that drove him to act as he did. What his father taught him made it difficult to establish a healthy relationship with any woman. As a Christian, he had much to unlearn.

Our church was his schoolroom for learning the heart's true desire and what it means to do things right in matters of the heart. Upholding a biblical vision of mature manhood and womanhood is part of the great work of a local fellowship and one of the life-changing benefits of belonging. This brother was maturing.

One Enduring Relationship

Pornography is a multibillion-dollar industry. Ninety-nine percent of it is a male viewing experience. Given the money pornography generates, you can be sure that if women wanted to view it, more would be produced. Men have a lust for pornography. Men in general also have more sexual partners throughout their life than women do. They engage in sex at an earlier age than women do. Men commit adultery more than women do.[10] How then can

---

[10]These are the conclusions of the major sex study, "The National Sex Survey," published by the University of Chicago (1992) as analyzed by Linda Waite and Maggie Gallagher, *The Case for Marriage* (New York: Doubleday, 2000), 78–96.

I argue that men desire a healthy, tender, passionate, enduring, mutually satisfying relationship with *one* woman?

The sociologist George Gilder points the way in his book *Men and Marriage*. He writes, "Under most conditions, young men are subject to nearly unremitting sexual drives, involving their very identities as males. Unless they have an enduring relationship with a woman—a relationship that affords them sexual confidence—men will accept almost any convenient sexual offer."[11] The key here is "unless they have an enduring relationship." Gilder argues that boys will be boys *until* they find the one enduring love they really need.

Men are more susceptible to the sins of promiscuity than women at precisely that time when they are *not* focused on establishing a healthy, tender, passionate, enduring, mutually satisfying relationship with one woman. Once a man sets his heart on such a relationship, the same male energy that once was casting about looking for mere copulation becomes a drive to woo and win, to care for and endure, and to provide and protect a woman and the children they have together. Of course, Shakespeare always knew this:

> Base men being in love have then
> a nobility in their nature more than is native to them.[12]

Mason Work for Men

So I think it crucial for us to make some distinctions. We must make a distinction between what the culture assumes we all want and teaches us to want, and what we really want. We must make a distinction between what we thought we wanted, merely to please others, and what we are truly designed to want. We must make a distinction between what we want as sinners in a sinful world, and what we want as men made in the image of God for great purpose. This is mason work for the soul.

[11]George Gilder, *Men and Marriage*, (Gretna, LA: Pelican, 1989), 11.
[12]Shakespeare, *Othello*, 2.1.218.

If there is a difference between men and woman in this matter, I think it is more that women know sooner, and long before it appears, what is the true and deeper desire of their heart. Men are hardly aware of it until struck or awakened by one particular woman. Then what the heart truly wants comes into focus. We want a healthy tender, passionate, enduring, mutually satisfying relationship with *one* woman. I offer four points of evidence.

1) Me

It is what *I* want. When I take Wendy Shalit's self-test, the results are not any different from when women take it. "Do [I] secretly long for a whole series of [women], to arbitrarily marry one of them and then maybe have affairs, maybe not—to be cool and wait and see if anyone better comes along, and then divorce—or do I long for *one enduring love?*" (author's emphasis). I want one enduring love. I want to live my life as a one-woman man.

Am I a minority? Probably, but who really knows. A friend mentioned to me recently that India is only 2 percent Christian. Then he reminded me, "That is no small number. It represents *twenty million* people." The same is true here.

Is this normal?

"What about when you were a teen?" someone might wonder. "Were you not a boiling pot of raging hormones? Did you not have, how shall we say it, more *normal* desires?"

I would say I had mixed desires, and they were a bit at war with each other. I had a strong curiosity, but I had an equally strong sense of modesty. This modesty was not shyness on my part (well, perhaps a bit) but a sense of protecting the young girl I was smitten with. It was because I liked her that I was particularly careful not to say, let alone do, something that might give her reason to draw back.

This, I propose, is normal adolescence. It is natural, meaning "as God made us to be." Young men are nervous, shy, and modest around women. Everyone's well-being is served by it, and women, especially, are safer. It is the abnormal experience of early exposure to porn or some form of sexual abuse that strips this away. Sexual desire lies dormant, sleeping in a way, until the proper season, unless awakened prematurely. Then it often becomes a lust, and women are less safe. The "boys will be boys" term, then, is too kind. It really means they have become predators. Many will object to the term, because they reserve this only for rapists or child predators. Still they are predators. They are not looking for a life partner. They are seeking out willing and foolish women for sexual recreation.

During my mid-teen years, like most, I became aware of the stunning images of pornography and my own lusts. If God had not touched my life at seventeen as a high schooler and made me sensible of his will, I'm sure the college scene would have torn away any remaining modesty and unleashed the lusts within. But again, this only confirms that I am a sinful man subject to temptations, and an insecure man subject to the need for peer approval. This need for approval from others (in the Bible it is called *the fear of man*) is the point of entry for most sin. It is the breach in our nature by which sin recruits and makes new disciples. Of these recruiters, Romans 1:32 says, "Though they know God's decree that those who practice such things deserve to die, they not only do them but give *approval* to those who practice them." It is the hunger for this approval that seduces us.

Before I had a chance to capitulate, God touched my heart. I knew almost immediately that God had a better way for me to go. When it came to women, that plan was for me to love one woman for one lifetime, till death do us part. It was a compelling vision.

2) You

You would not be reading a book called *Doing Things Right in Matters of the Heart* if you were not disposed toward the very same desire. You want to do things right and are curious about what that is. You may have come to this desire out of a past of unbridled lust and a series of relationships in which you discovered that that well does not hold water. Or you may, like me, simply want to learn "how to live in order to please God" (1 Thessalonians 4:1 NIV). When I tell you that in matters of the heart this means loving one woman faithfully, passionately, and tenderly and caring for her well-being even more than your own—doing so throughout all the "frowning providences" that come through a life endured together till death bids you to say goodbye—you are not surprised or put off. God has fit you for this purpose. It echoes within as a compelling and desirous vision for your life. Like me, you just need to learn what God has said about bringing it to pass.

3) God

When I say that men are made to love one woman for a lifetime, I am saying that this is how God designed us, the corroding effects of sin notwithstanding. Genesis 2:24 says, "Therefore a man shall leave his father and his mother and *hold fast to his wife*, and they shall become one flesh." This is the language of paradigm. Finding and taking a wife is for men of every culture in every age. This pattern will continue until the Lord's return. And it will end only because all marriages point to and are consummated in the one eternal marriage of Christ and his bride, the redeemed of every age who put their trust in him (Matthew 22:30).

One reason we can know that all men are "fit" to love one woman for one lifetime is found in the word "therefore." "Therefore a man shall . . . hold fast to his wife." It points back to Adam, the first man, and implies, "Adam did such and such. *Therefore*, all men will do such and such." Adam holding fast to his wife is God's created paradigm for all men in matters of the heart.

The details leading up to this *therefore* are worth noting. In Genesis 1:28, God declares that man will "be fruitful and multiply and fill the earth and subdue it and have dominion." In the next chapter, we discover how these purposes were set in motion. We learn that man and woman were not created simultaneously but sequentially. Adam was created first. Eve was not made until Adam understood how she was to fit into his life as a wife and coregent in the world. Genesis 2:18 sets up the lesson: "Then the LORD God said, "It is not good that the man should be alone; I will make him a helper fit for him." But what follows is not the creation of Eve but the naming of animals and birds. "Now out of the ground the LORD God had formed every beast of the field and every bird of the heavens and brought them to the man to see what he would call them. And whatever the man called every living creature, that was its name" (2:19).

In naming things, Adam is learning the nature of things and how they fit together. This is the beginning of science. In naming the animals and the birds, Adam becomes the father of zoology and ornithology. I assume he is also the father of ichthyology and geology and mineralogy, of oceanography, astronomy, and more. He understands the nature of the animals, so some are beasts and others, livestock (2:20). Here is the beginning of taxonomy and all varieties of species, with their phylums and orders, classifications, and families. In naming things, Adam is also exercising his authority over the rest of creation. And after a while, he gets the point! There is nothing in all creation that shares his nature, place, and purpose in the world. "But *for Adam* there was not found a helper *fit* for him" (2:20).

Wow!

The woman was created to fit him. Adam, after surveying all and finding only interesting things and weird things and dangerous and useful things, is finally presented with the *wow* thing!

> "This at last is bone of my bones
> and flesh of my flesh;
> she shall be called Woman,
> because she was taken out of Man." (2:23)

More simply, "This seems a great fit!" Or to speak plainly, "Wow! This is what I have been looking for!"

Therefore, men ever since have been following this pattern. By God's good design, rather than by sin's effects, we leave home and labor to find our place and purpose in the world till we hit the *wow*. Then we marry that girl and take on the world together.

God is in all this. He set it up this way and is still sovereign over whom we meet. I love how this is expressed in the song *Hello, Young Lovers*.

> I know how it feels to have wings on your heels,
> And to fly down the street in a trance.
> You fly down a street on the chance that you meet,
> And you meet not really by chance.

Whoops!

Doesn't the Bible portray polygamy as normal? Yes, it does. It also portrays divorce as normal. Greed, lying, pride, oppression, and death are also normal in the sense they are faithfully recorded in the Bible as the effects of human sinfulness and rebellion against the norm set down by God. These are all mankind's *whoops* where we have swerved off the path and created for ourselves new norms of painful consequences. Redemption is God saving us from our *whoops* and restoring back to us our original *wow*. This is the great work of the gospel.[13] So it is true that polygamy was normal in the sense that it was *common*. It was never normal in the sense that God designed us for this as a norm. It is never prescribed by God, only described by God (first in Genesis 4:19) as one of the painful patterns emerging from our rebellion to his rule.

When it comes to biblical prescriptions we find God protecting this one great purpose for men and their sexuality by a variety of warnings and reminders. "Flee from sexual immorality" (1 Corinthians 6:18); "For this is the will of God, your sanctification:

---

[13]For a full explanation of the gospel and our human experience of God's outworking grace, see John Ensor, *The Great Work of the Gospel*, (Wheaton, IL: Crossway Books, 2006).

that you abstain from sexual immorality" (1 Thessalonians 4:3); "Let marriage be held in honor among all, and let the marriage bed be undefiled, for God will judge the sexually immoral and adulterous" (Hebrews 13:4); "Sexual immorality and all impurity or covetousness must not even be named among you, as is proper [fitting] among saints" (Ephesians 5:3); "Can a man carry fire next to his chest and his clothes not be burned? . . . So is he who goes into his neighbor's wife; none who touches her will go unpunished" (Proverbs 6:27, 29); "You shall not commit adultery" (Exodus 20:14).

Therefore, we read of Joseph fleeing Potiphar's wife after she cast her eye on him and said, "Lie with me" (Genesis 39:7). We read of Job's passion to be faithful to his wife, "I have made a covenant with my eyes; how then could I gaze at a virgin?" (Job 31:1). In Proverbs 31:10 we are reminded what it is we are truly looking for: "An excellent *wife* who can find? She is more precious than jewels." And we are commanded to keep steering our affections toward this great find. "Husbands, *love* your wives" (Ephesians 5:25). A steadfast love for our wives alone reflects the steadfast love of God. Or to put it in the words of Shakespeare:

> Love is not love
> Which alters when it alteration finds,
> Or bends with the remover to remove;
> O, no! it is an ever-fixed mark,
> That looks on tempests and is never shaken;
> It is a star to every wandering bark . . . [14]

4) Shakespeare

My final piece of evidence that men, like women, are designed for one great love in the context of marriage is Shakespeare. I leave Shakespeare for last, not because he is more authoritative than God and his Word, but because he seems to be the ultimate testimonial to the wisdom and glory of God in Scripture regarding

---

[14]Shakespeare, *Sonnets*, 116.2.

matters of the heart. Shakespeare comes after God in the sense that "Praise be to God!" follows "Great is the LORD, and greatly to be praised" (Psalm 145:3).

Shakespeare catalogues all matters of the heart—pride, jealousy, revenge, betrayal, and, of course, love, that arise between us. And he affirms what Adam learned:

> He is half part of a blessed man,
> Left to be finished by such as she;
> And she a fair divided excellence,
> Whose fulness of perfection lies in him.[15]

Pressed too far, this is not true. Single people are fully human and live full lives. Lovers, however, routinely feel that they complete each other in deep and profound ways. However fit two lovers feel, though, Shakespeare knows that love is severely tested by life's providences. "The course of true love never did run smooth."[16] How that course twists and turns is the substance of his art. Shakespeare knows love's humor, its combativeness, its *eros*, its jealousies, its tragedies and triumphs. Shakespeare is Adam in naming all the matters of the heart. And by appealing to Shakespeare, I mean to use him as something of the "Adam" of all artists. Poets, song writers, novelists, painters, sculptors, filmmakers, and other artists all attempt through their art to search out the mystery called in Proverbs, "the way of a man with a maiden" (30:19 NIV).

What do they say? They testify that men can and do love deeply and singularly, as women do. If it were not so, the arts would not exist. Because it is so, and because we know it to be true, we believe Romeo when he wishes himself a glove:

> See! How she leans her cheek upon her hand:
> O! that I were a glove upon that hand
> That I might touch that cheek.[17]

---

[15]Shakespeare, *The Life and Death of King John*, 2.1.437.
[16]Shakespeare, *A Midsummer Night's Dream*, 1.1.132.
[17]Shakespeare, *Romeo and Juliet*, 2.2.23.

Because men love deeply and singularly, we believe it plausible that Romeo could break with his family and, no matter the danger, plot to be with his Juliet.

In Victor Hugo's *Les Miserables*, we know why Marius is ready to leave the French Revolution. He laid his eyes on Cosette. In Hugo's *Hunchback of Notre Dame*, we understand why Quasimodo rings the bells and fights off all of Paris. It's for his Esmeralda. Because we understand that a man *can* love one woman for a whole lifetime, we empathize with Quasimodo when he scoops up his dead Esmeralda, embraces her, and weeps, "Oh! All that I have ever loved!"[18] We are left satisfied, even feeling a bit triumphant in this tragedy's conclusion, when we read how many years later, Quasimodo's skeleton is found, bones bent and deformed. But wait! They are wrapped around the bones of another—the scooped up bones of his Esmeralda, whose side he never left. If men could not love singularly, this ending would be dismissed as farce rather than delighted in as a testimony of devotion.

The fact that men can and do love like this explains why Johnny Cash (1932–2003) got clean and sober and fought every day to stay that way. Johnny found his June (1929–2003). Through his art he testified:

> I keep a close watch on this heart of mine
> I keep my eyes wide open all the time
> I keep the ends out for the tie that binds
> Because you're mine, I walk the line.[19]

Because it is true that men can and do love singularly, Joe Cocker (1944–) sang:

> You are so beautiful to me, can't you see.
> You're everything I've hoped for; you're everything I need.
> You are so beautiful to me.[20]

---

[18]Victor Hugo, *The Hunchback of Notre Dame* (New York: Barnes & Noble Classics, 2004, orig. 1831), 647.
[19]Johnny Cash, "I Walk the Line" (1956), Sun Records.
[20]Joe Cocker, "You Are So Beautiful" (1975).

If this were not true, we would scoff rather than buy it by the millions.

Casablanca, considered one of filmmaking's greatest achievements, would not have, as one of its most famous lines, Humphrey Bogart's (1899–1957) character, Rick, lamenting his one true love, "Of all the gin joints in all the towns in all the world, she walks into mine." This providence rings true because we know it is true that we men can carry one woman in our hearts wherever we go, down through many years. And what is the single most beloved and celebrated cinematic musical score in history? It is Gene Kelly (1912–1996) splashing and "singin' in the rain." Art that is false at heart does not last, let alone become the apex of an art form.

What is more, each of us could quote poems, stories, songs, and movie lines that affirm the same thing and rarely duplicate the source, so abundant do the arts point to the true desire of the human heart. Women want a healthy, tender, passionate, enduring, mutually satisfying relationship with a good man. And men want the same with a good woman.

Chapter Three

What the Heart Lacks

In courtesy I'd have her chiefly learned;
Hearts are not had as a gift but hearts are earned ...

W. B. YEATS

I have seen among the simple,
I have perceived among the youths,
a young man lacking sense.

PROVERBS 7:7

When Percy Sledge sang his plaintive, now-classic ballad of 1966, *When a Man Loves a Woman*, he was merely declaring again what has been forever known. Men, like women, can love deeply, intensely, almost crazily.

When a man loves a woman
Can't keep his mind on nothing else
He'll trade the world
For the good thing he's found ...

To love a woman deeply, however, is not the same thing as loving her well and steadfastly. That experience is high achievement in this troubled world. To my disappointment, that is not what Sledge's ballad is about either.

Instead of describing how a man in love is guided towards maturity as a man, a husband, a lover, a father, and a friend, Sledge's lyrics turn inward to describe how burdensome, even ruinous, loving a woman can be.

> When a man loves a woman
> Down deep in his soul
> She can bring him such misery
> If she plays him for a fool
> He's the last one to know
> Lovin' eyes can't ever see[1]

Instead of an ode to one enduring love, this is a complaint: "She done me wrong! She played me like a fool!" Something is lacking here.

What the Heart Lacks

In the same way that hunger alone tells us nothing about eating nutritionally, our passions and urges do not teach us about loving well. We can be driven by the chemistry of creation to meet and greet but that is not the same as having a grasp on who we are meeting and what their needs are. Hormones and oxytocin bond us to those with whom we share a bed, but what it means to love beyond merely making love does not come from chemistry; it comes from theology. It comes from parenting. It comes by learning. Proverbs 19:2 says, "Desire without knowledge is not good." So let us take stock of what the heart lacks and see what needs to be added to desire if we are to do things right in matters of the heart.

---

[1]Percy Sledge, "When a Man Loves a Woman," Atlantic Records, 1966.

The Heart Lacks God

The philosopher Schopenhauer (1788–1860) believed that the quest for love, our heart's desire, was nature's little trick to perpetuate the species. Whatever personal and individual experience is at work in love is merely a ruse, by nature, by way of the sexual impulse, to fulfill nature's desire to reproduce and extend itself— the species search for eternal life you might say. "Nature can only attain its ends by implanting a certain illusion in the individual, on account of which that which is only a good for the species appears to him as a good for himself, so that when he serves the species he imagines he is serving himself."[2]

This is a bummer of a philosophy, if you ask me. Besides not answering why nature should prefer extension over extinction, or how it came to prefer it, the idea of being a pawn of some metaphysical force's quest for eternity is about as appealing as a bowl of canned peas for breakfast.

Augustine (354–430) took another tack. In his *Confessions*, Augustine concluded that his sexually reckless and wanton life was, in truth, a misguided search for everlasting happiness, and that this search for happiness was, in truth, a search for him who is Everlasting Love and Infinite Joy. "Thou hast made us for thyself, O Lord, and our heart is restless until it finds its rest in thee."[3]

I'll go with Augustine on this one. Our endless search for happiness explains just about everything we do, good and evil. We look for sex and drink beer because it makes us happy almost instantly. We repeat this because it is a fleeting happiness and so must be sought again and again. We go to college because it makes us happy to think of ourselves someday in business, medicine, education, or some other work we feel passionate about. We may hate chemistry or English literature, but we endure the classes in exchange for a latter and larger happiness. We may not be happy to pay our electric bill and rent, but we figure we are happier with

[2]Schopenhauer, "The Metaphysics of the Love of the Sexes," *The Philosophy of Schopenhauer* (New York: The Modern Library, Vol. 52, 1928), 346–47.
[3]Augustine, *Confessions*, 1:1.

lights and an apartment than without them. We strive to excel in whatever we do because of the ultimate happiness of life achievement. We seek a mate and desire children for the same reason. Even suicide is motivated by a sense that we will be happier dead than alive. In all these things we are in the search for happiness.

Augustine discovered that God is the happiness we seek; all else are mere pointers. "*Every* good gift and *every* perfect gift is from above, coming down from the Father of lights with whom there is no variation or shadow due to change" (James 1:17). If the gifts are good, how much more is the Giver? "For *he* satisfies the longing soul, and the hungry soul *he* fills with good things" (Psalm 107:9). He is the End of every desire. Apart from him all desires leave us thirsting for something more, something different, something new, something *else*.

Putting First Things First

When it comes to doing things right in matters of the heart, the first right thing we can ever do, the one right thing we must do, in order to get all the other things right, is to give our hearts to God. "*Love* the LORD your God with all your heart and with all your soul and with all your might" (Deuteronomy 6:5). If you ask me how to love God, I say, "*Seek* the LORD and his strength; seek his presence continually!" (1 Chronicles 16:11). "*Ascribe* to the LORD the glory due his name; *worship* the LORD in the splendor of holiness!" (Psalm 29:2). "*Glory* in his holy name; let the hearts of those who seek the LORD *rejoice*!" (1 Chronicles 16:10). "*Commit* your way to the LORD; trust in him, and he will act" (Psalm 37:5). "*Trust* in him at all times, O people; *pour out* your heart before him" (Psalm 62:8). "*Sing* praises to God, sing praises!" (Psalm 47:6.) "*Incline* your ear, and *come* to me; *hear*, that your soul may live" (Isaiah 55:3). This and more is what it means to love God.

Loving God first as a matter of the heart puts all our other loves in their rightful place and in their right proportion. We pursue them not as we will but according to his Word—seeking to do things right as a matter of trusting God to provide us with good things. And he will; that is his promise.

> Do not be anxious, saying, 'What shall we eat?' or 'What shall we drink?' or 'What shall we wear?' For the Gentiles seek after all these things, and your heavenly Father knows that you need them all. Seek *first* the kingdom of God and his righteousness, and all these things will be added to you. (Matthew 6:31–33)

First Love

Our first love must be God, through faith in the living Christ. If you wonder what this looks like, think of marriage. In Jeremiah 31:33 we read, "I will be their God, and they shall be my people." This is very close to saying, "I will be your husband and you will be my bride." It is the language of covenantal marriage. We find it again in Isaiah 62:4–5:

> You shall no more be termed Forsaken,
> and your land shall no more be termed Desolate,
> but you shall be called My Delight Is in Her,
> and your land Married;
> for the Lord delights in you,
> and your land shall be married. . . .
> And as the bridegroom rejoices over the bride,
> so shall your God rejoice over you.

These are marriage vows of sorts. God's delight in his Bride causes him to plan and pursue us just as a man pursues the one great love of his life. This in turn becomes the model or example for what we are after in our own intimate relationship. For example, we read in Ephesians 5:25–27, "Husbands, love your wives, *as Christ loved the church and gave himself up for her*, that he might sanctify her, having cleansed her by the washing of water with the word, so that he might present the church to himself in splendor, without spot or wrinkle or any such thing, that she might be holy and without blemish." We shall return to this again. For now it's important to see that our first longing, our first love, must be Christ. We were made for him, and to him we pledge our troth. "Grace be with all who love our Lord Jesus Christ with love incorruptible" (Ephesians 6:24).

The Idolatry of Idyllic Love

If we do not seek our happiness in God and make him our perfect and everlasting happiness, then every good thing becomes a substitute for God; it becomes an idol. I am thinking particularly of the common practice of pursuing human love and romantic relationships as the one great passion of our lives. Do this, and you place a burden on it that it can never bear. This is what happens in romanticism and idyllic love. The idealism and romanticism found in so many paperback romances and films reflect our search to find our eternal happiness in a human relationship. But idyllic love is a false pursuit. It is a mirage; it is a phantasm.

Idyllic love is pornographic in the sense that it presents a relationship as we idealize it rather than as it comes. In pornography love is idealized as sexual satisfaction without intimacy, friendship, or obligations. It is not real. In romance novels it is idealized as intimacy, friendship, and manly sacrifice and suffering, with no body noises or smells. This, too, is unreal.

Idyllic love is idolatry because it places on a man what only God can provide. No man can fulfill the deepest longings of the human heart because these longings belong to God alone and cannot be filled by another. Our desire for a healthy, tender, passionate, enduring, mutually fulfilling life with a good man or woman will always be a work in progress. There is no perfect marriage, only two people pledged to live together for better and worse. The best lover is still a sinner. As Shakespeare said:

> Roses have thorns, and silver fountains mud;
> Clouds and eclipses stain both moon and sun,

> And loathsome canker lives in sweetest bud.
> All men make faults . . .[4]

Sisters, to look to any man to be your all-consuming delight is to set him up for failure, and then you will hate him for disappointing you. You will find what you are seeking only in Christ.

Forever Young

Likewise, brothers, there is no eternal bliss in breasts. God green-lights our attraction in no uncertain terms:

> Let your fountain be blessed,
> and rejoice in the wife of your youth,
> a lovely deer, a graceful doe.
> Let her breasts fill you at all times with delight;
> be intoxicated always in her love (Proverbs 5:18–19).

But as Shakespeare says, "Everything that grows, holds in perfection but a little moment."[5] Finding another pair of breasts and then another as we grow older is a false pursuit of eternity, the quest to be forever young. This too is idolatry. God is the wellspring of our life. "In him we live and move and have our being" (Acts 17:28). "They who wait for the LORD shall renew their strength" (Isaiah 40:31). In him alone, are we forever young.

The Heart Lacks Discretion

The heart is big on desire, but it lacks discretion. Discretion is moral knowledge and moral judgment. Discretion is God at work in our heart, giving us the means to fulfill our heart's desire by first protecting us against fraud. Discretion is a defense system, a sorting system, weeding out the false and standing watch for you. "Discretion will *watch* over you . . . *delivering* you from the way of evil, from men of perverted speech, who forsake the paths of

---

[4]Shakespeare, *Sonnets*, 35.2.
[5]Shakespeare, *Sonnets*, 15.1.

uprightness to walk in the ways of darkness, . . . whose paths are crooked, and who are *devious* in their ways" (Proverbs 2:11–15).

The woman who lacks discretion is defenseless when it comes to fraudulent love. Sadly, the worst kind of man is often the best at seduction. They know what to say and are bold to say it. Godly men are often hesitant and halting. The predator flows with talk of love and oozes with sensuality. Predators are devious in that they appear to be conforming to your agenda, when they are merely wearing you down to the point where you conform to their agenda. They are there to conquer and consume. Sister, you'd better get discretion or buy Kleenex in bulk.

I Don't Know

A beautiful, single woman came to see me at our pregnancy center. She was finishing her doctorate at a prestigious Boston area university. She was smart and professional—and frightened. To her relief, she received a negative pregnancy test. I used the occasion to get to the heart of the matter.

"Do you mind if I ask you why you are sexually active right now?"

Her answer stunned me. I have since found it to be the most common answer to the question. She replied, "I don't know."

It was a moment of self-awareness for her. "I can't believe I am doing this, and I don't even know why!"

She knew why she was in graduate school. She knew why she was pursuing a career in medicine. She perceived herself to be a rational and thinking person. But here was a whole part of her life that she had not thought through. She was simply floating along on the currents of the age, and doing as everyone else did. She was paying a painful price for lacking discretion.

Poking Fun at Frauds

Without discretion you fall prey to the dimwitted notion that you are ready for sex when you are in love. Nothing is more typical and nothing is more wrong. Get discretion and you will know that *love* is consummated in *marriage*, not in intercourse.

> Love and Marriage
> Love and Marriage
> Go together
> like a horse and carriage . . . [6]

This truth did not go out with the horse and carriage. Love tacks toward marriage. *Covenanted* love, not the mere feeling of love, is ultimately celebrated in the free and wild embrace of sexual passion.

Sisters, without discretion, you conform to the practices around you. With discretion comes a little rebellion against the status quo, a little nonconformity. Without discretion sex is merely Elmer's glue for making things stick. With discretion comes insight into the value of *unmet* sexual desire in guiding a man towards the kind of healthy, tender, long-term relationship that is your heart's desire.

Without discretion you are in danger. With discretion the best of predatory men are easily spotted and defeated. They are rendered a joke.

"Haven't I seen you someplace before?"

"Oh yes, that's why I don't go there anymore."

"Hey girl, what's your sign?"

"Do not enter."

"I would go to the end of the world for you."

"Ah, yes, but would you stay there?"

There are a thousand of these floating on the Internet. They reflect the disarming power of a discerning woman.

If I've Told You Once . . .

The man who lacks discretion is equally brainless and defenseless when it comes to seduction. Discretion will watch over you . . .

---

[6]Sammy Cahn, "Love and Marriage," 1955.

So you will be delivered from the forbidden woman,
from the adulteress with her smooth words,
who forsakes the companion of her youth
and forgets the covenant of her God. (Proverbs 2:16–17)

I remember stumbling onto the book of Proverbs when I was
twenty years old. I was amazed at two things right away. First
were the urgent, repeated, pleading appeals to get wisdom and
discretion. "My son, be attentive to my wisdom; incline your ear
to my understanding, that you may keep discretion" (5:1–2). For
ten chapters these appeals are made! Here is a case where a loving
heavenly Father is saying, "If I have told you once, I have told you
a thousand times!"

Get wisdom; get insight;
do not forget, and do not turn away from the words
    of my mouth.

Do not forsake her, and she will keep you;
love her, and she will guard you.
The beginning of wisdom is this: Get wisdom,
and whatever you get, get insight.
Prize her highly, and she will exalt you;
she will honor you if you embrace her.
She will place on your head a graceful garland;
she will bestow on you a beautiful crown. (4:5–9)

We are charged to go after wisdom like Captain Jack goes for
treasure.

My son, if you receive my words
and treasure up my commandments with you,
making your ear attentive to wisdom
and inclining your heart to understanding;
yes, if you call out for insight
and raise your voice for understanding,
if you seek it like silver

> and search for it as for hidden treasures,
> then you will understand the fear of the LORD
> and find the knowledge of God. (2:1–5)

We are promised that in finding wisdom there is a very great reward:

> Blessed is the one who finds wisdom,
> and the one who gets understanding,
> for the gain from her is better than gain from silver
> and her profit better than gold.
> She is more precious than jewels,
> and nothing you desire can compare with her.
> Long life is in her right hand;
> in her left hand are riches and honor.
> Her ways are ways of pleasantness,
> and all her paths are peace.
> She is a tree of life to those who lay hold of her;
> those who hold her fast are called blessed. (3:13–18)

The second thing that amazed me about Proverbs was that its first major point of practical application was aimed directly at my sex life:

> My son, be attentive to my wisdom. . . .
> that you may keep discretion. . . .
> For the lips of a forbidden woman drip honey,
> and her speech is smoother than oil,
> but in the end she is bitter as wormwood,
> sharp as a two-edged sword. (5:1–4)

Get wisdom and discretion, or by default, you will be a moth to the flame! Then come the rather graphic consequences:

> O sons, listen to me,
> and do not depart from the words of my mouth.
> Keep your way far from her,
> and do not go near the door of her house,

lest you give your honor to others
and your years to the merciless,
lest strangers take their fill of your strength,
and your labors go to the house of a foreigner,
and at the end of your life you groan,
when your flesh and body are consumed. (5:7–11)

Here is the father-son talk of all talks. "Miss this, and you are dead meat, boy. That powerful urge within you will either be channeled into one enduring and precious love or it will drag you off, strip away all you cherish, and when you are left with nothing but yourself, it will eat away your flesh! Can a man play with fire and not be burned? Discretion, get discretion!" Yes, Father.

The Heart Lacks Customs

Brothers, there was a time when, if your father, your uncle, the preacher, or your coach saw you moving in the wrong direction, they would speak up and warn you about things, thereby giving you discretion. Sisters, you would have heard from your mother, your best friend's mother, an aunt, a Girl Scout leader, or a camp counselor. In some societies, they made harsh and cruel examples of "fallen women." Today we are not as cruel, though silence when someone is being led to the slaughter emotionally is cruelty of another kind. We are silent now because that is all that is left after postmodernity enshrined *choice* and *making your own truth*.

Up until now, matters of the heart were guided by traditions and customs deeply rooted in the culture. There were well-defined codes and expectations about how one went about pursuing a love interest—courtship rules that guided the process along. A proper introduction had to be made. Parents approved a suitor. The young woman knew that suitableness for marriage was the point of it all. Chaperones offered a level of protection against youthful passions.

For centuries chivalry was a code, defining how men were to treat women. In later periods there was the *gentleman*. Being a gentleman meant dutifully protecting a woman's honor and chastity and serving her as the "weaker vessel" (1 Peter 3:7). A gentleman, by the virtue of the title, knew something about doing things right in matters of the heart.

These codes and customs are lacking now. They were destroyed because they were judged oppressive to women. Now women are free from what have come to be viewed as the quaint, belittling protections of chivalrous men. Women are now equal, so they are no longer weaker. Or are they? Wendy Shalit writes,

> I was born in 1975, and from anorexia to date-rape, from our utter inability to feel safe on the streets to stories about stalking and stalkers, from teenage girls finding themselves miserably pregnant to women in their late 30s and early 40s finding procreation miserably difficult, this culture has not been kind to women. And it has not been kind to women at the very moment that it has directed an immense amount of social and political energy to "curing" their problems.[7]

Tradition Is Not Enough

Tradition, however, is not without error and often has been full of error. Like every marriage, every culture in every age has certain blind spots. In Victorian England, for example, women had few options in life except whom they were to marry. As this one decision, more than any other in their lives, determined the economic conditions for the rest of their lives and that of their children, it was no small matter.

Since all people are sinners, all the traditions arising from people are partly good and partly corrupt. In their worst use, traditions protect the systemic public sins of the age—India's traditional caste system, Europe's upper and lower classes, America's slavery and child labor practices, etc. Traditions played a role in limiting the rights of women to vote, own property, get an education, and more.

---

[7]Wendy Shalit, *A Return to Modesty*, 8.

We ought not to delude ourselves that we are no longer bound by traditions. Indeed, traditions become binding very quickly these days. You can identify them simply by the pressure you feel from others and by asking yourself what will bring you approval from your peers. The most often used reference to describe our traditions today is probably *political correctness.*

In making the case that we lack customs, my point is not that the old ways were good and the new ways are bad. It is that many of the old customs and codes, particularly in matters of the heart, were benign and beneficial, and today they are gone. In their time, they greatly assisted men and women in knowing how to approach one another and what to expect in the realm of relationships. We are now lacking such cultural cues.

Feminism's answer to the lack of customs is for women to take the initiative. Be aggressive and just go up to him and say, "Will you go out with me?" Such things almost never work in real life. So women ready to pursue matters of the heart are largely left with happenstance and kismet. It makes for a lot of waiting and frustration.

Courtship customs in earlier days provided intentionality for both men and women. A father, or a couple with young adult children, approached other families to make introductions and arrangements. At the extreme, some cultures have arranged marriages. They have a surprisingly good record for producing healthy, tender, enduring relationships. I scoffed at this tradition one day when a Christian couple from a different culture scoffed at the American dating game. Theirs was an arranged marriage, and they were proud of it. They ticked off all the chaos of our custom-free culture. They praised their parents for wisely taking matters into their own hands, rather than leaving them at the mercy of kismet. They spoke passionately about how their parents had brought them together and how their marriage was truly a marriage of two families. I was impressed.

The apostle Paul advised, "I would have younger widows

marry, bear children, manage their households, and give the adversary no occasion for slander" (1 Timothy 5:14). I take this to mean that something *active* is appropriate in regard to young women finding a good man to marry, have children, and establish a home.

In spite of feminism's hostility toward women who have marriage as their heart's desire, it is a common desire and one to be greatly cherished and respected. It says nothing about limiting a woman's role to only that of a wife, but it does imply more than happenstance and kismet in obtaining it. Arranged marriages and courtship customs are never coming back into our culture, but this does not mean that a woman cannot turn to her father, or that a young man can't turn to a couple in his church, to see if some arrangement can't be made for an introduction and a time for interaction amidst a larger group. A mature elder or deacon, a grandfather or uncle—any of these could be a great help. Churches do well to plan for interaction.

The Heart Lacks Examples

A young woman in my church told me that she had never dated a man she hadn't slept with. "Why?" I asked.

She said, "That's the way my mother does it. That's what all my friends do. They see it as just part of dating."

"Are any of them happily married?" I asked. None were. In fact, there wasn't anyone in her family, even in her extended family, who was married. Her mother had never married. Her sisters and brothers had children but no spouses. She had no models for doing things right in matters of the heart. She had no father to show her the way and to protect her along the way.

In contrast, I am the only condom my daughter will ever need. I am her protection. I have modeled for her what kind of man to look for in marriage by how I live and love her mother. I have shown her what to look for—someone who values integrity and lives in submission to God, someone who works hard for his family and laughs loud with them and can't keep his hands off his wife. My boys too are watching and learning from me.

Sorta Like Me

I used to put my daughter to bed with a prayer. I would pray for her and ask God's blessing on her future life. Then I would pray for her future husband as well. I prayed for him as a little boy to find God's will for his life and to grow up to be a godly and good man.

When I was done I would ask her, "What kind of man do you want to marry some day?" Then I taught her the answer as well: Someone just like me!

Sweeter words were never heard from a grinning daughter than "Someone just like you, Papa!" Of course I don't think she will want someone *exactly* like me. "Sorta like me" will do fine. In other words, I am her model for what kind of man she is looking for.

The Family Circus

When models are lacking, what do we do? I grew up in a home where my father was alive but gone. He left the home at 7:30 AM. He worked from 8:00 AM till 5:00 PM. Then he drove to a tavern. He came home after I was long in bed, somewhere around eleven o'clock to midnight. At 7:30 in the morning he was gone again. I was seventeen years old and hanging out with a family in my church, the Olberg family, before I realized that some fathers ate dinner at home and hung out all evening with family. The kids were zany, the parents were caring. Together they were guiding, advising, rebuking, and loving. They simply lived as a family. I simply absorbed.

It was my turn to learn, and my local church was providing the lessons. Models of good marriages are books in clothes. The church was my library.

The Heart Lacks Confidence

The androgynous, asexual, gender-bending, role-reversing view of modern egalitarianism is so unattractive to me that I cannot help but think most of us publicly embrace it simply because it saves time and bother when we are in public. It is all so much "bar talk." Bar talk is my reference for the way in which people will agree with someone's forceful political opinion when sitting in a pub. No matter how asinine it might be, those at the bar will say, "Yep. You got that right, Bud." They agree because they are there to drink, not think. Privately they think something else, but why bother?

So it is with the inverted role expectations of so much of modernity. I wonder how many true converts there are. I must admit, though, that it has rendered men and women unsure of what it means to be a man or a woman, and it has made men and women insecure about how to relate to each other.

Women lack confidence in their desire to be a wife and mother. It is acceptable as a side dish, but should it be the main dish, something must be wrong with them. Men who want to do the right thing toward women are now unsure if it is okay even to open a car door for them.

Since most American cars now do not have a keyhole on the passenger side door, men are being told in no uncertain terms that chivalrous door-opening is out of style. In our sterile environment, a man merely pushes the key fob and the woman opens her own door. These small assaults on the cultural cues that help define manhood and womanhood have produced paralysis. Men are afraid to do the wrong thing when they should be confident in knowing and doing the right things.

Wimps for Jesus!

The majority of the people who attend Park Street Church in Boston are college and graduate students from Harvard, MIT, Boston University, and other prestigious institutes of higher learning. I once addressed about two hundred of these students at a weekend retreat. I was a little nervous about one point I wanted to make. In talking to them about matters of the heart, I wanted to hit the issue of male confidence and manly initiative straight on. I worried that I might be in for some chauvinist-pig-type responses. Nonetheless, seeing so many men hesitant and fearful about matters of the heart, I let fly, "Brothers, God did not call you to be wimps for Jesus!"

All the women burst out with clapping. I have little doubt that many of them were feminist or egalitarian in their thinking. Nevertheless, they were beyond frustration by the lack of boldness and confidence in the men around them.

As for the men, they laughed as well. It was as if they were let out of the stall. It was one of those "the emperor has no clothes moments" where everybody saw it but nobody dared say what he or she really thought. Instead they had been trained what to see and said only what was expected. In truth, the brothers had always wanted to charge ahead, but they need someone to say, "Men! See that? Go get it!" They had it within them to do this, but lacked confidence given the whole male-female "rigamarole" that now pervades sexual politics.[8]

In the two years that followed, close to a dozen couples approached me and said they met at that retreat. It made me feel mighty pleased. Two years later they are filling up the nursery for Jesus.

The Heart Lacks a Good Foundation

We do not lack information about how all our parts work. That has been covered pretty well in every public school over the last thirty years. Insert part A into part B. Make sure part A has attachment C. If attachment C fails, part D will result. If so, pay X amount to the people who sold you part C and they will remove part D. All very basic and sterile if you ask me. Such information is not the foundation we lack.

What we lack is a biblical foundation for matters of the heart. I think most of what God has to say about it can be fairly summarized as follows.

---

[8]This phrase comes from Andree Seu, "Rigamarole" *World* magazine, (March 25, 2006), 47.

*1) What we desire and describe as a healthy, tender,
passionate, enduring, mutually satisfying relationship,
God simply calls marriage.*

Genesis 2:24–25 says, "A man shall leave his father and
his mother and hold fast to his wife, and they shall become
one flesh. And the man and his wife were both naked and
were not ashamed." As I hope to show you in the following
chapters, when the Bible speaks of two becoming one flesh,
it is pointing towards the unity of body and spirit that mark
a healthy, tender, passionate, enduring, mutually satisfying
relationship.

Adam and Eve were husband and wife, naked and unashamed.
This hints at passion, of course, but also at the health that belongs
to a marriage. There was no guilt, no shame, no woundedness,
no intrusive memories of previous partners to cope with (okay,
this one wasn't possible, but it sure is now). When Christ read
these words, he saw God at work and thus an enduring quality in
marriage: "What therefore God has joined together, let not man
separate" (Matthew 19:6).

First Peter 3:7 points to the tenderness required of husbands and reminds them that the goal of their behavior is the
wife's honor and satisfaction in the partnership. "Husbands,
live with your wives in an understanding way, showing honor
to the woman as the weaker vessel, since they are heirs with you
of the grace of life, so that your prayers may not be hindered."
Biblically based marriages bear the marks of tenderness and
mutual satisfaction. The point is that what we are after is marriage as God wills it to be. The poet John Donne (1572–1631)
hit the same point hard:

> Who ever loves, if he do not propose
> The right true end of love, he's one that goes
> To sea for nothing but to make him sick.[9]

---

[9]*Elegy 18*, "Love's Progress".

*2) The most modest single people make the most
   passionate married people.*

We are commanded to flee sexual immorality and to run from adultery because God desires for marriage an unfettered intimacy that is unstained by promiscuity.

> Drink water from your own cistern,
> flowing water from your own well.
> Should your springs be scattered abroad,
> streams of water in the streets?
> Let them be for yourself alone,
> and not for strangers with you. (Proverbs 5:15–17)

Sexual purity outside of marriage makes for sexual passion within marriage. Since it has all been reserved for one, it is now released in full. God devotes one entire book, the Song of Solomon, to paint this picture of marital love. Husband and wife are exclusive and singular in their passion. "As a lily among the brambles, so is my love among the young women" declares the lover (2:2). She echoes back her unfettered sexual delight reserved for him: "As an apple tree among the trees of the forest, so is my beloved among the young men. With great delight I sat in his shadow, and his fruit was sweet to my taste" (2:3).

It is descriptive and poetic rather than graphic. It is full and free passion under the banner of their covenanted love.

> While the king was on his couch,
> my nard gave forth its fragrance.
> My beloved is to me a sachet of myrrh
> that lies between my breasts.
> My beloved is to me a cluster of henna blossoms
> in the vineyards of Engedi. (Song of Solomon 1:12–14)

All other sex is less than this, because it is sex without love, sex without truth, sex without concern, sex without commitment, sex without fidelity. But from a biblical standpoint, marital intimacy promises the fullness of human sexuality.

The corollary was summed up well by C. S. Lewis (1898–1963). The Christian rule is "either marriage, with complete faithfulness to your partner, or else total abstinence."[10] To protect the enchantment of *eros*, intimacy is highly protected.

According to the Bible, sexual intimacy is, first, the consummation of covenanted love. It declares the unity of body, soul, and spirit that God has created in the marriage. If a child is conceived, there begins a literal expression of two halves becoming one flesh. It is not a question of sex being designed for recreation or for procreation; it is about unity, about two becoming one flesh, in brief moments of ecstasy, and in the creation of a living legacy of marital love.

3) Marriage is not for quitters.

It is for keeps. It is forever (Matthew 19:1–12). Therefore, marriage is not to be "entered into lightly or unadvisedly." It is for keeps because marriage is a covenant made between two people *and God*. Just as we do not want God to break his covenant with us, so he does not want us to break our covenant with him and with our spouse. As God is a promise keeper, so we are to be promise keepers. Admitting that marriages need work to succeed is only to acknowledge that marriage is a labor of love. It is not for cowards or quitters.

Divorce, then, is as much an enemy to our heart's happiness as pornography. It is a loathsome reality. Yes, it happens. So does rape. That is how we ought to look at it. Divorce hurts. Divorce violates. Divorce leaves people broken. Do I know people who have divorced? Many. Have they recovered? Some. I also know a few who have been sexually violated and then recovered. But they don't ever minimize it or wish it on anyone.

In our nearly thirty years of marriage the word *divorce* has

---

[10]C. S. Lewis, *Mere Christianity* (San Francisco: HarperCollins, 2001, orig. 1952), 95.

never been spoken between us. Discussing divorce would be as strange as if I were to say, "Babe, let's call the bank and tell them to just keep our money." Or if she were to say, "John E., I think I will fly off to Tuscany for a muffin." *What?* That is the strangeness we have made of divorce. Could it happen? Of course. But it will not happen if we are both seeking for each other a healthy, tender, passionate, enduring, mutually satisfying relationship. Is our relationship always this way? Of course not. Therefore, we keep seeking after God and asking to be filled with his Spirit. We give ourselves to the labor that love requires, and we do this because divorce is not an option.

What's Past Is Prologue

Sexual immorality, adultery, divorce—these are common sins and leave a lasting sting. Looking into God's Word and seeing the clarity of his righteous laws can leave us groaning under the burden of our past. So let me remind you that the very first thing we ever really do right before God is to confess our waywardness, admit our guilt, and cast our cares onto Christ. He is our righteousness. That is why the gospel comes as "good news of great joy" (Luke 2:10).

So I would ask you not to become defensive about your past in reading about God's will for your life. Agree with God and rejoice in the grace of God. Nothing is lost in Christ. "What's past is prologue," Shakespeare reminds us.[11] It all works for a greater good, to our joy, and to his glory. Pray, "It is good for me that I was afflicted, that I might learn your statutes" (Psalm 119:71). Say with the Bard:

> O benefit of ill! Now I find true
> That better is by evil still made better;
> And ruin'd love, when it is built anew,
> Grows fairer than at first, more strong, far greater.[12]

---

[11]Shakespeare, *The Tempest*, 2.1.261.
[12]Shakespeare, *Sonnets*, 119.9.

Chapter Four

What's at the Heart of Manhood and Womanhood

We know of no culture that has said, articulately, that there is no difference between men and women except in the way they contribute to the creation of the next generation.

MARGARET MEAD

Do not be conformed to this world, but be transformed by the renewal of your mind, that by testing you may discern what is the will of God, what is good and acceptable and perfect.

ROMANS 12:2

Winston Churchill said, "It is a riddle, wrapped in a mystery, inside an enigma."[1] He was trying to understand Russia. He should have been talking about the mystery that now faces us.

---

[1] Radio broadcast, October 1939.

Three things are too wonderful for me,
four I do not understand:
the way of an eagle in the sky,
the way of a serpent on a rock,
the way of a ship on the high seas,
and the way of a man with a virgin. (Proverbs 30:18–19)

There is much mystery in matters of the heart. Geoffrey Chaucer (1343–1400) takes up the theme in *The Canterbury Tales*. One tale involves a knight whose life is forfeited to a woman. She tells the knight, "I will grant you life if you can tell me what thing it is that women most desire." The man soon realizes that his doom is merely delayed:

He sought in every house and every place
Where he hoped to find favor,
In order to learn what thing women most love;
But he reached no land where he could find
two people who were in agreement with each other
    on this matter. [2]

Nothing has changed since Chaucer wrote this around 1387. We continue to wrestle with the mystery of it all. "Why can't a woman, be more like a man?"[3] Will Mars and Venus clarify what it means to be one and not the other? Why is it that no one wants to even ask for clarification? Wendy Shalit expresses her frustration, writing,

"The best predictor of someone's future behavior is their past behavior," warns *YM* magazine in 1998. This is what used to be known as a *reputation*. All the questions a woman might wonder when it comes to the man she's about to become involved with—Is he moral? Is he good? And does he know what it means to be a man?—have

[2]Geoffrey Chaucer, *The Canterbury Tales*, ed. A. Kent and Constance Hieatt (New York: Bantam, 1964, orig. 1387–1400), 223.
[3]Frederick Loewe and Alan Jay Lerner, "Why Can't a Woman Be More Like a Man?" in *My Fair Lady*, 1964.

been reduced to this. For we are not supposed to care if he's moral (who knows what's moral?), or if he's good (who knows what's good?), and above all we are not allowed to ask if he knows what it means to be a man. That, of course, would be extremely uncool because that would be sexist. One cannot ask about male honor because male honor is supposed to be oppressive to women. Every woman of my generation knows this—we learned it with our ABC's.[4]

Here we are, facing the most important matter this side of heaven, shrouded in the greatest mysteries, and women are not permitted to freely ask certain basic questions. This is not good! It's time for a little nonconformity! The key questions we should be asking openly and confidently are "What does it mean to be a man and not a woman?" and "What does it mean to be a woman and not a man?" This gets us very near the heart of the matter.

The Illusive Perfect Match

When I survey the many couples I know who have a healthy, tender, passionate, enduring, mutually fulfilling life with one another, they all look extremely different: loud and quiet, argumentative and differential, gregarious and reserved, homebodies and travelers, or messy visionaries and detailed with everything labeled and in its place. Healthy marriages appear quite possible in all the mixing and matching of personality types on the DISC personality test.

The couples I know hold in common what appears to be a clear appreciation of who they are as men and women and what role they are called to in the marriage. They may chafe at it a bit; they may wear on one another, but knowing what it means to be manly or womanly pushes them to do the right thing and creates a unity of spirit, which is the heart of marriage itself. We may freely affirm much mystery "in the way of a man with a virgin" (Proverbs 30:19). However, that means that what can be understood should be underscored all the more.

---

[4] *A Return to Modesty*, 8.

Take the Archetype, Leave the Stereotype

Genesis 1:27–28 (NIV) is the beginning of what can be known about male and female:

> God created man in his own image,
> in the image of God he created him;
> male and female he created them.

God blessed them and said to them, "Be fruitful and increase in number; fill the earth and subdue it. Rule over the fish of the sea and the birds of the air and over every living creature that moves on the ground."

Here is the archetype, not the stereotype, of manhood and womanhood—not what we are because of sin, but what we are by creation. Here is what we have fallen *from* because of sin. Here is what we are being restored *to* through the outworking grace of God through our faith in Christ. What does it tell us? What is at the heart of manhood and womanhood as created by God?

A Clear Appreciation of Our Equality

From Genesis 1:27–28, we gain a clear appreciation of our equality as men and women. We are, first off, equally created *by God*—"male and female he created them." What is more, God creates them both in a distinct fashion from the rest of creation. All other parts of creation God calls forth in an indirect fashion: "Let there be . . ." (1:3, 6, 9, 14). In making man and woman, God acts *directly*, "God created. . . ." Herein lies the inherent dignity of all human life; we are, as male and female, his special creation.

The substance of that special dignity comes next. Men and women are equally made as image bearers of God: "in the *image* of God he created him; male and female." I would think that this is blessing enough, but there's more. Men and women were equally *blessed* by God in their creation: "God blessed them and said. . . ." This is important to remember, because it is the basis of our moral obligation, equally given to men and women, to trust in God. This blessing reveals the benevolent character of God towards us. He did not wind us up as toys, let us go, and then retreat to play elsewhere. He created the man and the woman, blessed them, provided abundantly for their needs (1:30), and implemented a definite plan and purpose for both. His blessing reveals the loving nature of his rule and points to the infinite obligation we have to love him for it, to acknowledge his sovereignty, and to praise him for his goodness (see Romans 1:21). All this we share equally.

His blessing also points to what is at the heart of all his prohibitions and directives. When God prohibits something, he is not robbing us of a good time. He is preserving for us a *better* time. He is blessing us, and this blessing is for both men and women equally.

Good and Plenty

Men and women are equally commissioned to be prosperous, to be fruitful in their labors at home and in the world: "God said to them [both], 'Fill the earth and subdue it'" (1:28). We are not potted plants. We are not house cats with nothing much to do but lick ourselves till we are tired and then take a nap. We have purposeful work to do. In this we reflect God as a workman. He worked six days in creation and took satisfaction from it: "and God saw that it was good" (1:10, 12, 18, 21, 25). He created man and woman with a double delight: "it was *very* good" (1:31). In Hebrew, it is literally, "good, good," or as we might say, twice as good. He commissioned them both to fulfilling labor.

This labor comes in two spheres. We have families to build ("fill the earth") and a world to manage ("subdue it"). We labor in bearing and rearing children. We labor in the world around us, in large measure to provide for our family members and to prepare them to go out into the world to further fill it and subdue it. We pass along to them the blessing of God's benevolent rule. We pass on the infinite obligation to live for the glory of God and forget not all his benefits.

Subduing the earth is the other sphere of fulfilling labor. We labor to harvest wheat and prune vines for our daily bread and jam. Beyond these needs, however, we also labor to create and build, as God did, for the satisfaction of it. We beat iron into nails, break rocks into gravel, mine gypsum into sheetrock, saw pine into house beams, till soil for corn seed and study its properties to discover further uses of it, build factories to make new products discovered from it; we ship, stock, sell, and account for it all, get paid for our labor, and then spend it on the fruits of other people's creative labors, such as the Internet and iPods. Each generation builds on the labors of previous generations.

Finally we may add that men and women are equally called to reign over all else God created: "Rule over the fish . . . and the birds . . . and over all the creatures that live along the ground" (1:26 NIV). Men and women together serve as coregents of the earth, to fill it, subdue it, unlock its secrets, and be good stewards of its resources. This, too, is part of what it means to be in God's image. For God is the ruler over all things.

Partners in Crime and One in Christ

Then there is the rest of the story. Men and women are equally rebellious against the rightful rule of God over their lives. We are equally born with a sinful nature that expresses itself as self-centeredness and self-will. We equally hurt and are hurt as self-centeredness works itself out in our relationships. We are equally wayward and wounded.

Men and women are, as a result of sin and rebellion, equally cut off from the love of God by their sins and under his fearful wrath for the evil that they do. Men and women are equally hopeless to fix this problem by themselves. We are altogether like Jonah, sinking down and doomed apart from a very providential encounter with a big fish that can both swallow and belch. We are alike rescued from a sin-driven life to one that is pleasing to God by the great work of the gospel. We are equally forgiven and remade into God's image and likeness through repentance and faith in Christ. We share jointly in the outworking of God's grace. We are co-heirs of the kingdom of God (1 Peter 3:7). Indeed we can say that before him, "there is no male and female; for [we] are all one in Christ Jesus" (Galatians 3:28).

Without this appreciation of our inherent equality, most people consider themselves either superior to those of the opposite gender or inferior and unworthy of decent and honorable treatment. We resent every slight and putdown. Women are apt to manipulate men as a means to an end—money, security, power, influence. Men are apt to reduce women to playthings, at worst demeaning them as "bitches" and forcing them into obsequious servitude. Any hope for doing things right in matters of the heart must begin with a clear appreciation for our equality of value and dignity as men and women created by God in his image.

A Clear Appreciation of Our Complementarity

From Genesis 1:27–28 we also learn that men and women are distinct and different from one another. God created us as male beings and female beings. We were created not identically but symmetrically. At the heart of mature manhood and womanhood is a clear appreciation of our complementarity.

Our differences are real and profound and good. Herein is the mystery of attraction unfurled. He cries:

> But, soft! What light through yonder window breaks?
> It is the east, and Juliet is the sun![5]

She proclaims:

> When he shall die,
> Take him and cut him out in little stars,
> And he will make the face of heaven so fine
> That all the world will be in love with night,
> And pay no worship to the garish sun.[6]

---

[5]Shakespeare, *Romeo and Juliet*, 2.2.1.
[6]Ibid., 3.2.21.

Here we are point and counterpoint. *Viva la difference*! But what does this mean? We do not understand our complementarity. We do not realize that we are wired for different types of reactions. With no effort at all, we misunderstand and frustrate each other to no end. But with understanding, we can also learn to complement each other.

The New Taboo

"The obsolescence of masculinity and femininity—of sex roles and of heterosexual monogamy as the moral norm—have diffused through the system and become part of America's conventional wisdom," writes George Gilder.[7] Yet with universal agreement, biology, psychology, and anthropology record clear and distinct differences.[8] Where gender differences are acknowledged, they are far from appreciated. Instead they are considered remnants of patriarchy that by nature are unjust and oppressive. All differences are considered imbalances, and imbalances must be corrected and made equal. Equal makes things fair. To be fair, masculinity and femininity must be deconstructed. A new androgyny must be created and then imposed. I can hardly wait.

The alternative is to find wisdom and appreciation in the differences and to make the most of them. That is my purpose here. I want to sketch out and illustrate a few of our differences just to confirm your suspicions that you are seeing things correctly and to underscore how good they are. Having a clear appreciation of both our equality and our complementarity defines our distinctive contributions toward building a healthy, tender, passionate, enduring, mutually fulfilling life as men and women.

[7]George Gilder, *Men and Marriage* (Gretna, LA: Pelican, 1989), viii.
[8]For excellent surveys of these differences with exhaustive documentation see Michael Levin, *Feminism and Freedom* (New Brunswick, NJ: Transaction, 1987), 70–97; George Gilder, *Men and Marriage*, 19–28; John Piper and Wayne Grudem, *Recovering Biblical Manhood and Womanhood* (Wheaton, IL: Crossway, 2006), 280–331; Stephen E. Rhoads, *Taking Sex Differences Seriously* (San Francisco: Encounter, 2004).

We Complement Each Other in Our Primary Interests

Men show themselves to be oriented toward and to have a primary interest in the mastery of the external world. Women tend to be oriented toward and to show a primary interest in the mastery of relationships. This is a blessing from God.

"God blessed them and said to them, "Be fruitful and increase in number; fill the earth and subdue it" (Genesis 1:28 NIV). Our primary interests correspond in complementary ways to the two spheres that God ordained for purposeful and satisfying labor—filling the earth and subduing it. We are equally commissioned to be fruitful in our labor at home and in the world around us. But we complement one another in the proportion of interest and satisfaction we gain from laboring in the two spheres. Women are stronger than men in establishing hearth and home. They have a primary interest and draw a double portion of satisfaction in the well-being of their marriage, in their children, and, by extension, in promoting peace and stability within the community.[9]

God has chosen not to dispense the labor of childbearing equally to men and women. He has made it the specialty of women. He has correspondingly not further burdened women with having to "subdue the earth" in equal measure to men. Rather, he has made it the primary interest of men. In this men and women complement one another. Does this mean that women do not work outside the home? No more than it means that fathers do not instruct their children. No, it means they fill the earth and subdue it in different and corresponding measures. And it means that this is a relief and a blessing to both.

XY Is Not XX

As each of us has a primary and secondary role in the well-being of the family, our chemistry corresponds to each of the spheres in larger

---

[9]An example of this is found in Abigail's efforts to promote peace when violence was about to break out in her town of Carmel (see 1 Samuel 25).

and lesser amounts. Men have fifteen times more testosterone than women. For this reason, men are generally stronger and sweat more. This is good for men when they are out subduing the earth. Women have ten times the amount of estrogen, which gives them greater endurance. They can endure more pain, and they live longer. This is good for women when they are bearing a child and raising it.

Men score higher in levels of aggression, dominance, and self-confidence. Women score higher in levels of nurturance, empathy, and intimacy. Men take more chances and die sooner. Women are more cautious and stabilize their environment, creating longer life for all. Men are more direct and linear in their speech and reasoning, less concerned about the impact on others, whereas women are more indirect and connective. Men seek competition to greater degrees than women. Women seek cooperation in higher degrees then men. Men consistently score higher in math, science, and economics. Women score higher in philosophy, human relations, and verbal skills.

Why these differences should be so threatening is hard to grasp. The issue is not about equality—equality is a given. Nor is it about superiority and inferiority. It is about men being stronger than women and women being stronger than men in different and complementary ways. Our complementarity is rooted in nature.

Making Trees Grow Sideways

What differences in male and female are nurtured and what come by nature is an old question and the subject of massive amounts of ongoing research. There is much mystery in the intersection of nurture and nature regarding manhood and womanhood. You can raise boys to be masculine and girls to be feminine (and I think we should). You can also raise effeminate boys and aggressive girls. The current cultural effort toward androgyny has made more progress than I would have guessed. With constant pressure you can also make a tree grow sideways. But is it natural? And is it attractive? Do you want a whole forest of them? I doubt it. It's interesting for about five minutes. Then the oddness of it all gets in the way and the sadness of it kicks in. In the same way, women won't look long for effeminate men; the old virile type will still do quite nicely. And men are still attracted to beautiful and feminine women. We hunger for something that complements us. As James Thurber (1894–1961) said adroitly, "I love the idea of there being two sexes, don't you?"

A Compelling Vision of Manhood and Womanhood

Appreciating our essential equality and complementarity as male and female image-bearers, John Piper has drawn up a working vision statement for manhood and womanhood. Piper attempts to answer the core question, what does it mean to be a man and *not* a woman and vice versa? He writes of manhood:

> At the heart of mature manhood is a sense of benevolent responsibility to lead, provide for, and protect women in ways appropriate to a man's differing relationships.[10]

He writes of womanhood:

> At the heart of mature womanhood is a freeing disposition to affirm, receive and nurture strength and leadership from worthy men in ways appropriate to a woman's differing relationships.[11]

Piper chooses his words carefully in forming this definition. He takes pains to explain their meaning and implications carefully.[12] He makes no claim that his definition is perfect in the sense of being complete. Perhaps it is not completely accurate in all that it attempts to say. There remains a mystery in manhood and womanhood. But Piper's vision statement is helpful at pointing us toward much of what can be known.

---

[10]John Piper, *What's the Difference?* (Wheaton, IL: Crossway Books, 1990), 19.
[11]*What's the Difference?* 35.
[12]To read Piper's full explanation, go to http://www.cbmw.org/rbmw/rbmw.pdf.

Adam's Role in the Matter

This vision for mature manhood and womanhood appears to me an accurate distillation of the picture provided for us in the Bible. In Genesis 1:27 we read:

> God created man in his own image,
> in the image of God he created him;
> male and female he created them.

Here is the first clue that man is called to lead and to act on behalf of the relationship in a way that women are not. God creates man in his image, that is, both man *and* woman, while at the same time signaling that the male is divinely called upon to serve in a way that the female is not. In other words, it is meaningful that this verse does not say, "God created woman: in the image of God he created *her*; male and female he created them."

God's use of the word *man* in Genesis 1:27 is referred to as the generic use. The word *man* is often used in Scripture this way, as in "man does not live by bread alone but man lives by every word that comes from the mouth of the LORD" (Deuteronomy 8:3). The English poet John Donne said,

> No *man* is an island, entire of itself . . .
> any *man's* death diminishes me, because I am
>   involved in mankind;
> and therefore never send to know for whom the bell tolls;
> it tolls for thee [italics added].[13]

We study this in English literature courses. It is perfectly understandable English. Yet in colleges today, if you wrote an essay on Donne's poem, you would be forbidden to use *man* in the generic case. Why? If the generic use of man is inherently inclusive, why exclude it? It is because the generic use of man refers to something

[13] John Donne, *Devotions upon Emergent Occasions*, 17.

more than shorthand for both sexes. It affirms the lead role of man in acting for both sexes.[14]

From a biblical standpoint this concept is called *headship* (see Ephesians 5:23). A man's inherent sense of headship, or leadership, is more fully developed in Genesis 2–3. The first pointer comes in the discovery that while man and woman were created equally, they were not created simultaneously. Man was created first (2:18) and the woman later. Some have suggested that by this reasoning the animals have authority over man because they were made prior to Adam. But that is not how Scripture reasons out the matter. 1 Timothy 2:13 calls for men to accept their leadership responsibilities, saying, "For Adam was formed first, then Eve." There is meaning in the order of creation, and it hints at male headship.

Adam's leadership is further revealed in his naming of things. In the process of naming, Adam comes to understand that he has no equal and no complement. There is nothing that is like him and that fits him as a life companion (2:18–20). Woman is then created from the man and for the man (2:23). His first act of leadership is to name her. This is an exercise of his headship, showing that he now understands the precious, wonderful gift he has received and is taking the lead in naming this gift in a befitting and honorable way.

This at last is bone of my bones
and flesh of my flesh;
she shall be called Woman
because she was taken out of Man. (Genesis 2:23)

---

[14]If the generic use of *man* is no longer acceptable, how will *mankind* survive? *Mankind* should probably be avoided since inherent in this word is still the idea that *man* has a preeminent role in standing for all people—male and female. There is not a linguistic equivalent in the word *womankind*. People take this to mean the sisterhood of all females. That is not fair because *mankind* does not mean just *men*. *Personkind* will have to do. But on second thought, perhaps not. Because that has the word "son" in it and that is gender-specific. So we must use the word *humankind*. Oops, that won't do at all, for *humankind* simply repeats the problem of *mankind*. And *huwomankind* is simply not going to catch on. I am sure, however, that those who reject the generic use of man are working on a solution.

That this leadership is benevolent in nature is seen in that he names her *wo*man—an extension of man that is equal to him and complements him.

Let Me Show You the Place

The man is given the moral and spiritual mandate about the tree of the knowledge of good and evil (2:16). He is expected to convey this to the woman later on. She is not told of it by God; she learns it from the man. He was responsible to lead her to an equal understanding of God's bountiful and free provision for them and his prohibition regarding eating fruit from the one tree in the garden.

Adam's leadership is further revealed in the fact that it falls to him to convey to the woman who God is (ruler over all), what he is like (benevolent), what he has said ("eat freely"), what he has commanded regarding the tree of the knowledge of good and evil, and what their disobedience will mean ("you will surely die").

"Honey, you see all this beauty around us?"

"Yes, dear."

"It is all ours to enjoy. God has made it for us."

"It is breathtaking."

"Yes, God is a mighty God—and he is very good. Do you see all these fruit trees?"

"Yes."

"God has said that we may eat *all* that we want."

"Praise be to God!"

"Yes, let us thank him and give him glory. But you see that one tree there?"

"Yes, it is beautiful as well."

"Yes, but God has commanded us not to eat from that *one* tree."

"Why?"

"I'm not sure. He hasn't told me yet. We'll just have to trust him that he knows best. One more thing, it was not given me as a request or a suggestion; it was a clear prohibition. The day we eat of that tree, we will die."

"Are you sure?"

"He said it twice—you shall surely die."

"I don't want to die. Thank you for protecting me."

"Hey, look at that! What name do you think would be fitting for it?"

Adam leads her to know God and his will. She joins him as a coregent in the world. For this reason Piper says that mature manhood carries within it a sense of benevolent leadership and that at the heart of mature womanhood there is a freeing disposition to affirm and receive it. Men are providers and protectors of women, and women are well served by it and glad to receive it.

A Recognition of Our Depravity

I have already underscored how we, as men and women, are equally sinners as well as image bearers. C. S. Lewis called us broken-down castles, but still castles. Here I would add that not only do we sin equally, but in complementary ways as well.

Sin first of all affects our growth. Mature manhood and womanhood are stunted by sin, which keeps us immature long into adulthood. Male leadership, twisted by sin, becomes distorted in every man. Depending on his personality and upbringing, sin will bend him toward running from his responsibility to lead, leaving him passive and timid, or bend him toward heavy-handedness, making him authoritarian and cruel.

The freeing disposition in womanhood, which supports and welcomes male headship, is equally distorted when twisted by sin. It either yields in a passive and disengaged way or it takes the lead and wrestles for control.

I Will Make Thee Think Thy Swan a Crow

In the story of the fall, the tempter says, to quote Shakespeare, "I will make thee think thy swan a crow."[15] Though Adam was the one to receive the moral mandate directly from God and was

---

[15]Shakespeare, *Romeo and Juliet*, 1.2.92.

responsible to teach it to the woman, the tempter, by way of the serpent, immediately usurps this order and approaches the woman. He said to the woman, "Did God actually say, 'You shall not eat of any tree in the garden'?" (3:1).

"Honey! There is a snake in my face!"

That might have worked as a good response if she had been at her best; it would have indicated her alarm. From what she had learned thus far about the world around her, about the *nature* of things gained through her work with Adam, she ought to have known that snakes don't approach; they generally slither away. And they don't talk! Something was amiss.

She might have yielded to the man, saying, "I was not there. If you want to know *exactly* what God said, ask him." From the text, we know that the man was not off climbing a coconut tree somewhere. He "was with her" (3:6).

Adam too ought to have noticed that among all he had studied and named thus far in the garden, he had not encountered talking serpents either. As the leader in this relationship, he might have stepped in.

"Excuse me. Did you *say* something?"

The serpent might have repeated, "Did God actually say, 'You shall not eat of *any* tree in the garden'?"(Genesis 3:1).

Adam might then have responded, "You could not be more wrong! God said we could freely eat from all the trees except one. What do you think: that God wants to starve us or something? That he is mean and holding out on us? Get out of here before I beat you with this stick!"

Instead, the woman takes the lead and the man follows her. She answers the serpent and gets confused about what God actually said. She increases the prohibition from "do not eat" by adding "neither shall you touch it" (3:3). She decreases the penalty for breaking faith with God from "you will surely die" to simply "lest you die" (3:3). In the process, she believes the serpent's suggestion that God is withholding his goodness from them and that God's laws are aimed at keeping them down and dumb (3:5). The serpent indeed turns their swan into a crow.

As an act of self-actualization (how modern!), she then takes the forbidden fruit and eats. Still leading, she gives the fruit to Adam. Adam, having already abandoned his role as leader and protector, follows her lead. "She took of its fruit and ate, and she also gave some to her husband who was with her, and he ate" (3:6).

The fall of man (generic use, of course) is not found in the eating of the forbidden fruit. The sin was breaking trust with God, confirmed in the eating of the forbidden fruit. It was believing that God was no longer good and was holding out on them. It was believing that their glad submission to God's rule was a form of oppression, preventing them from being all that they could be. By rebelling, they thought that they could be wise like God (3:5). Their sinfulness, as it related to each other, was in the man's failure to lead, provide, and protect and in the woman's taking the lead.

Adam, Front and Center!

So who is at fault? The man and woman are equally under God's judgment, and so they both hide from God. "The man and his wife hid themselves from the presence of the LORD God among the trees of the garden" (3:8). But because the man is the leader, he is more at fault. When God comes to judge them, he does not approach the woman, who took the lead. Nor does he call them both forward, though they share in the guilt. He approaches the man, because God still holds him accountable as the head of the household. "The Lord God called to the man and said to him, "Where are you?" (3:9).

We can confirm that we are right in our understanding because 1 Corinthians 15:22 says that in Adam's sin, we all have sinned. It is not in Adam *and* Eve's sin that we sin. Adam was not only the head of the family but also the head of the human race.

The War between the Sexes

From this we may be sure that in forming a healthy, tender, passionate, enduring, mutually fulfilling life with a good man or woman, we will, as sinful men and women, have particular sinful tendencies.

Brothers, our sinful nature will tempt us to follow Adam and yield our responsibility to provide godly leadership in our marriages and families. We are tempted to absorb ourselves in work and hobbies and become passive, disengaged fathers. We are apt to let her take matters into her own hands when it comes to teaching and disciplining the children and in conveying the moral will of God through Scripture reading, prayer, and worship. We even mask our laziness with feigned honor: "She is better at these things than I." If we take a passive role, we will have no vision for the family beyond buying things and having dinner and intercourse. God will hold us accountable for what comes from this.

On the other hand, our sinful nature may attempt to press us toward a demanding authoritarianism, a short temper, and an expectation that we are to be waited on. Controlling, argumentative, always angry—such men use fear rather than persuasion to settle all disputes. In the process, their wives shrink within and seethe with bitterness. Their marriage is doomed, and God will hold the men to account for the murder of it.

Sisters, your sinful nature turns a freeing disposition to affirm, receive, and nurture male leadership in one of two ways as well. It either tempts you, like Eve, to want the lead and to take control, or it will attempt to distort your inherent dignity and rob you of self-confidence. You will be fearful and obsequious in your relationships with men. The result is that you do many things you do not think are right or healthy. You will tolerate the intolerable because you are afraid to be without a man in your life. You will attach yourself to an immature man when you should be finding your hope and strength in Christ as his daughter first.

Our essential equality and our complementary callings are

distorted by sin. The result is four thousand years of recorded human history of the battle between the sexes: women usurping and manipulating, and men frustrating them at every turn. It is the stuff of both tragedy and comedy.

Shakespeare took up the battle in his *Taming of the Shrew*. Two strong-willed lovers, Petruchio and Katharina, fight a battle of wits and control. He will demand her servitude to his lordship:

> I will be master of what is mine own.
> She is my goods, my chattels; she is my house,
> She is my household stuff, my field, my barn,
> My horse, my ox, my ass, my anything.[16]

Kate swings from an unyielding will to a mocking subservience. Petrucio looks at the sun and says, "Good Lord, how bright and goodly shines the moon!" And she replies,

> Sun is not the sun when you say it is not,
> And the moon changes even as your mind.
> What you will have it nam'd, even that it is;
> And so it shall be so for Katherine.[17]

As the play ends they are starting to get it right. His love is bending him toward serving her rather than commanding her. Her love is softening her need to control or to pretend to be mindless. But you can see that the struggle will always be there.

In real life we too must learn to get this right. It is the labor of love.

---

[16]Shakespeare, *The Taming of the Shrew*, 3.2.231.
[17]Ibid., 4.5.20.

Doing Things Right

Chapter Five

Doing Things Right

In idle wishes fools supinely stay;
Be there a will, and wisdom finds a way.

GEORGE CRABBE

Trust in the Lord with all your heart,
and do not lean on your own understanding.
In all your ways acknowledge him,
and he will make straight your paths.

PROVERBS 3:5–6

There are many things we could use some help with in matters of the heart: how to fight fair, how to communicate better, how to change and grow without drifting apart, how to achieve mutual fulfillment in intimacy, how to divide the chores. None of these things do we get in Scripture. Instead, what we get is the heart of the matter: how to achieve unity, how two become one. The rest will work itself out according to personal preferences, gifts, and time.

For example, for many years I took responsibility to pay all the bills. Somewhere along the way, we realized that we were both a little happier when my wife took care of it. Since our communication was not always the best, this seemed one way to make sure we both understood just how much was in the tank. In other words, it was our sensitivity to what would lead to unity that helped us sort out who does what.

The heart of the matter is unity, two people becoming one. The wisdom and guidance we get from Scripture is that which promotes unity of spirit and shows how two very different people can move as one. This I intend to trace out in the following chapters. But first let me offer an illustration of what I think all the chapters add up to.

The Grit and the Gold

In the Winter Olympics, figure skating events are the hottest ticket in town. Pairs figure skating has occasionally been the highest-rated event among viewers. At its best, it displays the strength and beauty, the power and grace, of true unity. The gold medal is awarded to the couple who has most mastered the skills of male leadership and female support.

He leads her onto the ice and initiates each part of their routine. She receives that leadership and trusts in his strength. His raw physical strength is more on display than hers; he does all the lifting, twirling, and catching. She complements his strength with her own—a more diminutive and more attractive strength of beauty, grace, speed, and balance. His focus as the head, or leader, is to magnifying her skills. Her focus is on following his lead and signaling her readiness to receive his next move. He takes responsibility for the two of them, and she trusts his leadership and delights in it.

If he makes a mistake, she pays the larger physical price while he pays the larger emotional price. She falls, but he fails! So he has to learn to initiate and risk. She has to help him understand her moves and to endure his learning curve.

They do not fight for equality on the ice; they possess it as a given. Each has a role to play and they are not jostling or fighting about fairness. They are after something far more rewarding. No one yells, "Oppressor!" as he leads her around the arena, lifting her up and catapulting her into a triple spin. No one thinks she is belittled as she takes her lead from him, skating backward to his forward. No one calls for them to be egalitarian: "She should get to throw him into a triple Lutz half the time!" They complement each other in their complementarian approach to becoming one majestic and powerful whole. No one, least of all he, minds that the roses and teddy bears, thrown onto the ice when they have collapsed into each others arms at the end, are for her. It is his joy.

This appears to me to be a visible model of what male leadership and female support are all about. This is what it looks like as it is worked out. It is an art form, not a mandate. It is a disposition, not a set of rules. When it is done well, it is a welcome sight in which both partners are fulfilled in themselves and delighted in the other.

Olympic skaters would be the first to agree that this takes grit, practice, and patience. They trade in the currency of bruises, cuts, twisted ankles, and sore shoulders. But what they are purchasing is a unity of movement that they both fittingly rejoice in.

My wife and I used to remind our children, "Doing things God's way is hard. But remember, the Devil beats his own." We were reminding them that doing things right is not easy. Doing them wrong, however, is harder still to bear in the long run. So it is in matters of the heart. What follows is what I honestly think is the right thing to do in matters of the heart. It is what we must each do with practice and patience if we would build a healthy, tender, passionate, enduring, mutually fulfilling life with a good man or woman.

Chapter Six

He Initiates . . . She Responds

He: Do not you love me?
She: Why, no; no more than reason.
SHAKESPEARE

He: Behold, you are beautiful, my love;
behold, you are beautiful;
your eyes are doves.
She: Behold, you are beautiful, my beloved,
truly delightful.
SONG OF SOLOMON 1:15–16

I was speaking with a small circle of college students, Christian brothers in their mid-twenties mostly. One of them expressed the problem squarely. "I don't like to ask until I see all the right signals that she is going to say yes."

My response? "Coward! You are the *man*."

By this I meant to say that being a man means something distinctive.

Brothers, it falls to us to be the initial risk takers in matters of the heart. Headship means being the one to go ahead and ask.

It is ours as men to suffer the embarrassment of rejection if need be. It is our role to initiate. It is hers to respond with a signal of reception or rejection. Get to it right merrily.

We are the hunters. They are the quarry. It is for men to strike out into the forest and look. It is for women to crack the twigs and stir the leaves so we know where to find them.

The Timidity of J. Alfred Prufrock

T. S. Elliot (1888–1965) said, "There will be a time to prepare a face to meet the faces that you meet." In sports they call this "putting on your game face." In matters of the heart, it means going forth confidently to meet the faces that you meet. Then speak up.

> If I could write the beauty of your eye
> And in fresh numbers number all your graces,
> The age to come would say, "This poet lies;
> Such heavenly touches ne'er touched such earthly faces."[1]

Okay, maybe it won't spill forth with the eloquence of Shakespeare, and this might be too much at first. Still, it is yours to make the move, no matter how much the fear of rejection grips your throat and causes you to stutter. Play the man.

Brothers, if you are not persuaded, let me show you the future. T. S. Eliot's call to preparedness is part of his famous poem "The Love Song of J. Alfred Prufrock." It is an ode to *timid* manhood, marked by hesitancy and fear. Opportunity surrounds him; love is his to have and hold, but he fails to initiate. He sees her light brown hair and soft arms; her perfume captivates him. But he is filled with self-doubts and hesitancy:

> And I have known the arms already, known them all—
> Arms that are braceleted and white and bare

---

[1] Shakespeare, Sonnets, 17.5.

(But in the lamplight, downed with light brown hair!)
Is it perfume from a dress
That makes me so digress?
Arms that lie along a table, or wrap about a shawl.
And should I then presume?
And how should I begin?

Yes, he should presume, and no, he should not worry about how to begin. Just begin. He considers the issue again:

Should I, after tea and cakes and ices,
Have the strength to force the moment to its crisis?

Yes, he should have the strength to push the situation to the moment of decision. But he is timid where he should be bold. Failing to make the most of his opportunity, all he has now is a sense of his failure:

I have seen the moment of my greatness flicker.
And I have seen the Eternal Footman hold my coat, and snicker,
And in short, I was afraid.

The result is a sense of defeat not just in finding love but defeat in being a man:

I should have been a pair of ragged claws
Scuttling across the floors of silent seas.[2]

Don't let this be your love song. It is ours as men to risk by asking. It is theirs to respond with yes or no. It is ours to first expose our hearts. It is theirs to echo with their own interest and affection, *or not*.

The Power of the Echo

Sisters, all the advice from *Vogue*, *Glamour*, and *Cosmopolitan* that talks about going after and getting your man, all the blather about how in this day and age it is just as acceptable for you to

---

[2]T. S. Eliot, "The Love Song of J. Alfred Prufrock," from *The Waste Land and Other Poems* (New York: Harvest, 1962 edition), 3.

initiate as for him, is just that—blather. The proof is that it feels wrong. Be confident and trust your feelings on this matter. Be confident that if he is the man you hope and wish him to be, he will play the man. You crackle the leaves a bit when he is in the area and let him know you are there. Then wait for him to initiate, *or not*. In the long run, you will be well served either way.

Sisters, as the relationship unfolds, let him also be first to say, "I love you." His power is in the exclamation. Yours is in the echo. He proclaims:

> Behold, you are beautiful, my love;
> behold, you are beautiful;
> your eyes are doves. (Song of Solomon 1:15)

She echos:

> Behold, you are beautiful, my beloved, truly delightful. (1:16)

In Shakespeare's *Much Ado about Nothing*, Benedick does not want to be the first to say "I love you." He tries to elicit Beatrice to go first. She is wise enough to know her place and the power that it has. She will insist he play the man before she plays the woman.

> **Benedick:** Do not you love me?
> **Beatrice:** Why, no; no more than reason.
> **Benedick:** Why then, your uncle and the prince and Claudio have been deceiv'd; they swore you did.
> **Beatrice:** Do not you love me?
> **Benedick:** Troth, no; no more than reason.
> **Beatrice:** Why then, my cousin, Margaret, and Ursala, are much deceiv'd; for they did swear you did.
> **Benedick:** They swore to me that you were almost sick for me.
> **Beatrice:** They swore that you were well-nigh dead for me.[3]

And so the battle goes, till finally Benedick ends the matter by

---

[3]Shakespeare, *Much Ado About Nothing*, 5.3.72.

confessing his love and taking her into his arms. This is the right thing to do. And I think this is the way most women picture it. Trust the picture.

Challenging the Matter

I once had lively discussion with a brother who insisted that in his relationship everything was equal, and that this was the hallmark of their marriage. To him equal meant *same* and therefore *interchangeable*. He proudly rejected the idea of male initiation and female response. And what is more, he thought he was serving the cause of women in this.

I responded by saying that in my marriage, my wife and I never think about equality, though if forced to think about it we would affirm our mutual worth before God. Instead, I see my wife as better and more precious than I—of greater worth. And I told him my wife took no offense in this matter. Indeed she gets upset with me precisely at the point when I start treating her as my equal. To her it feels like a step down.

Then I gave him my pudding test. Here is where we compare what we think we believe to what we actually know and practice. I asked him, "Did you ask her out first or did she ask you out?"

He asked her out.

"Perhaps it means nothing," I said, "then again, it is curious. I suppose then on the second date you waited for her to ask you out?"

Well actually he had asked her out two times in a row—a disturbing imbalance to be sure!

I asked, "Do you think that she was taken by your handsomeness in equal measure that you were first taken by her beauty?"

"Probably not," he conceded, revealing a worrisome imbalance in what attracts men and women to one another.

Next I asked, "The decision to be sexually abstinent until marriage—did you first raise the matter or did she have to raise it first?"

He had taken the lead on the matter but insisted that they both equally agreed that this was the will of God for their lives. Very well.

Then I went for broke. "When it came to proposing, did you ask her or did she ask you?"

"I asked her," he conceded.

"Would it have been just the same if she had asked you? Or is it simply the right thing to do, simply more fitting for both of you, that you initiated the proposal and she responded to it?"

He said he was not sure and would have to think about it. He was sensing finally that something true and right was afoot here. He was seeing how in his actual life, rather than in the intellectual ideology that he espouses, he lives as I do. He actually was the initiator, and she was well served by it! He could sense that something would be amiss if she had proposed to him.

It does make a difference who takes the initiative and who responds. When it comes to doing things right in matters of the heart, men initiate and women respond.

Chapter Seven

He Leads . . .
She Guides

If ever wife was happy in a man,
Compare with me ye women if you can.
ANNE BRADSTREET

I will make him a helper fit for him.
GENESIS 2:18

*I*n matters of the heart, it is right that men should lead and women welcome and guide that leadership. She is his helpmate (Genesis 2:18). Her goal is to give her man all the help he needs to lead well. His goal is to humbly accept the responsibility to lead and not run from it or wield it like a club.

The guidance that she provides him comes mainly in two forms: in helping him *think clearly* and in encouraging him to *act confidently*. What comes from this is a shared victory. If it proves a mistake, it is borne together. Either way, what is fostered is true unity of spirit which is the heart of the matter, where the two become one. We have to work at it, but if we do, true unity is fostered and preserved in the complementary exchange of male leadership and female guidance.

Love Set to Normal Operating Mode

Brothers, in a sort of back-handed way, God deals with our sinful tendencies to avoid leadership and directs us around them when he says, "Husbands, live with your wives in an *understanding* way" (1 Peter 3:7). The *New International Version* of the Bible says, "Husbands . . . be *considerate* of your wives." I take this to mean we ought to lead with questions rather than conclusions. It means we ask about what she thinks is best, and we consider how she will be affected by the matter. Following this directive casts our whole leadership into the mold of tenderness and thoughtfulness.

Sweethearts thrive and blossom in such an environment. They do not feel as great of an urge to wrest control. They are more readily pleased to yield because they feel deeply and profoundly loved by thoughtfulness. It's a paradox worth remembering: when we are full of thoughts about their well being, they are filled to overflowing with love. Surely this is one of the mysteries between us.

Think of love as a setting on some gizmo. If love set on "high" is passion and love set on "low" is grinding out the work of reconciliation, think of consideration and understanding as love set on the "normal" operating mode. This is love as it operates routinely, day-to-day, through the ebb and flow of life.

Turn Up the Volume, Tune Out the Man

Sisters, you too have specific guidance on this matter. For example, Proverbs 21:19 says, "It is better to live in a desert land than with a quarrelsome and fretful woman." Proverbs 27:15 adds, "A continual dripping on a rainy day and a quarrelsome wife are alike."

This quarrelsomeness is the habitual critiquing of male leadership expressed in the tone and spirit of sarcasm rather than in respect for male leadership. It is how the good gift of female guidance expresses itself when twisted and controlled by sinful self-centeredness rather than by the Spirit and love. It harps and barks and nags and belittles the man and his position as leader.

Sisters, if you repeatedly attempt to control the man in your life, and if you disrespect him and the decisions he makes, you will get nothing for it but neglect and emotional abandonment. It is another of those mysterious paradoxes. There are plenty of witnesses to this truth all around—women who dismiss the biblical admonition, "let the wife see [to it] that she respects her husband" (Ephesians 5:33). Instead, they try to their ever-lovin' frustration to get their man to do what they think he should do—about every matter under the sun. But here is the thing: men naturally chafe and eventually flee from direct instruction from their wives. They do not change when you tell them to. And they never, ever will. When you turn up the volume, you tune out the man.

Love in the Indirect Mode

Instead, try *indirect* instruction. 1 Peter 3:1–2 says, "Likewise, wives, be subject to your own husbands, so that even if some do not obey the word, they may be *won* without a word by the conduct of their wives—when they see your respectful and pure conduct."

This is the way of a woman with a man. She teaches him primarily by example. When needed, she may appeal to his thoughtfulness and ask for his consideration, but she will not go further. He will be far more apt to give consideration to her words when they are heard as an appeal or a suggestion rather than as a directive. Think of it as the difference between casting a flashlight down the path versus pointing it in his face. Direct light causes us to close our eyes. Indirect light, pointed away from our eyes, causes us to strain to see.

When God instructs a man, he uses a direct approach. "Husbands, live with your wives in an *understanding* way" (1 Peter 3:7). Not all men obey this word, as Peter acknowledges in 3:1 ("if some do not obey the word"). Even when men desire to obey God's Word, their immaturity as men and as Christians renders them inconsistent, given to fits and spurts—mere seasons of obedience amidst times of hardness of heart. This is no doubt painful for women to bear.

Nevertheless, when God instructs women what to do about it, he tells them to continue to be submissive in spirit. It has its own power to soften a hardened heart over time. Pounding on him will only make him harder.

Respecting his leadership and guiding it this way also reflects a trust in God. It says, "I believe that God is at work in his life and mine." So let God, in his providence, bend the stiff neck of your husband, beat down his rebellion, soften his sharp edges, and fan into flame a vision for what it means to be a husband, father, and entrepreneur in the things of God. Until then, shut up about it in his presence. Turn it over to God, "casting all your anxieties on him, for he cares for you" (1 Peter 5:7). "Be still before the LORD and wait patiently for him" (Psalm 37:7).

Practicing toward Perfection

Most men are afraid to lead, as T. S. Eliot illustrated so well in his "J. Alfred Prufrock." Women have told me, "I have to lead because he won't." That may be sadly true and in some ways inescapable. However, it is more often true that there is a conspiracy of sorts going on. He is quietly afraid to lead and she is quietly eager to lead.

The wise woman will resist this impulse. She will simply leave some things undone and, instead of becoming bitter, she will respect her husband as he is while looking for ways to help him find his footing and be the leader that God wants him to be. The wise man will bear the responsibility to lead, even if he is utterly convinced and it is self-evidently true that she does a better job.

The first place all this is practiced is in planning dates. Generally, even though we have been married for nearly thirty years, my wife wants me to have a plan already in mind. She likes it when I lead.

Far too often I don't have one. Her response then is to let us wing it. She will not do the planning for me.

Another good time in which to practice leadership and guidance is after a disagreement. When my wife and I argue, when the relationship is torn, it is my role as a man to initiate the repair. She knows it, submits to it, and is glad to have it so. I must make the first move when we are both wounded and hesitant to do so. Why? Because headship means "go ahead." It means getting things started. That is my responsibility in the matter. If I fail at this moment, it would be akin to the lead skater dropping his partner on the ice. My wife would be hurt all the more, and I would be left with a wounded wife. What is the victory in that?

Likewise, my wife does not run off somewhere. She stays within reach, and she stays quiet. She knows what is going on. I am thinking and preparing and resisting and finally initiating the work of reconciliation.

United in Holding Our Noses

Another arena for this practice of headship and submission, of leadership and guidance of leadership, is in the context of having to decide things that have lasting consequences that are not easily reversed. It is for me to make the final decision when we are both uncertain or in disagreement about what is right. My wife will provide her best judgment and guidance: "Here is what I think . . ." or "We have to think about this factor or that." Then when she's done, she will add, "But you decide. God holds you accountable for it." Sounds a bit harsh, but it's true.

We are currently wrestling with a decision about where to reside. We have elderly parents to consider, changing ministry considerations, grown children now resettling all over the country, and the high cost of living in New England to cope with. One of the major options we are considering is most unappealing to my wife, but there are compelling reasons for us to consider it. I presented this option to her along with why I think it's a good one. She said, in summary, "I don't like it." A little later she added, "I will do it, if that is what you ultimately think is best." In the days that followed, she thought of several additional points for us to consider. She also did some research online. She was *helping* me make the final decision.

As for my part, I want to lead in a way that is considerate of her as 1 Peter 3:7 instructs me. So I proposed the "stinker" idea with a long lead time. I want her to have the time to adjust to it. If I am missing something, I want her to help fill in the picture. Most of all, I want us to be united in the decision, even if we are both holding our noses as we do it.

It takes practice, but it works. He leads, and she respects and guides his leadership.

Chapter Eight

He Works . . . She Waits

Ain't misbehavin'
I'm savin' my love for you
SUNG BY ELLA FITZGERALD

For this is the will of God, your sanctification:
that you abstain from sexual immorality;
that each one of you know how to control his
own body in holiness and honor, not in the passion
of lust like the Gentiles who do not know God.
1 THESSALONIANS 4:3–5

*D*oing things right in matters of the heart means that he works and she waits. Wendy Shalit calls this "male obligation and female modesty."[1] The insight here is to understand that there are certain things that come to women by *waiting* that only come to a man by *working*.

Even at the most intimate level this is true. The mutually

---

[1] *A Return to Modesty,* 102

satisfying experience of orgasm comes by a husband *working* and a wife *relaxing*. What is true at this consummation level of a relationship is also true at the foundational level. In matters of the heart, men are to work to win and women are to wait and be won. As Shakespeare said,

> She is beautiful and therefore to be woo'd.
> She is a woman, therefore to be won.[2]

The Transforming Power of Waiting

Sisters, this means reclaiming the power of modesty and chastity. Nothing will make a man work harder at wooing and preparing himself to wed than modesty and chastity. Men *work* when women *wait*.

Sociologist George Gilder asserts that the key force in society that transforms immature manhood into mature manhood is women's sexual self-control, her power to wait. Most men are driven toward sexual intercourse in ways that most women merely decide. Regarding this reality George Gilder says, "The fact is that women lack the kind of importunate, undifferentiated lust that infects almost all men."[3]

This is just one aspect of the complementary nature of male and female regarding our experiences as men and women. Though in general women can live more easily without sexual intimacy than men, their experience of it is longer and more satisfying than a man's. Men are sexual dots. Women are sexual lines. Men are sexual moments. Women are sexual minutes. Men erupt. Women are fanned into flame. What a complement! And it is vital to understand the implications of it.

Gilder continues, "The man may push and posture, but the woman must decide. He is driven; she must set the terms and conditions, goal and destinations of the journey."[4] Men may wield

---

[2]Shakespeare, *King Henry the Sixth*, 5.3.78.
[3]*Men and Marriage*, 11.
[4]Ibid., 12.

more power in the economy of the marketplace, but women control "the economy of the eros." He explains:

> Men lust, but they know not what for; they wander, and lose track of the goal; they fight and compete, but they forget the prize; they spread seed, but spurn the seasons of growth; they chase power and glory, but miss the meaning of life. [5]

Shakespeare said it with a little more flare,

> O! What men dare do! What men may do!
>   What men daily do!
> Not knowing what they do![6]

As for women, Gilder continues:

> In creating civilization, women transform male lust into love; channel male wanderlust into jobs, homes, and families; link men to specific children; rear children into citizens; change hunters into fathers; divert male will to power into a drive to create.[7]

How do women transform immature men into mature ones? Through the power of their modesty and chastity. Such women understand not only the moral clarity of God's Word, but they also see the wisdom in his commands to abstain. When women wait, the impatient male predator will go elsewhere, which protects them from the wrong man. The immature man, however, is forced to consider what changes in his life need to be made. He asks, "What are the terms and conditions under which I may turn your 'Not now' and 'Not yet' into 'Let my beloved come to his garden and eat its choicest fruits!'" (Song of Solomon 4:16). Then he gets to work and grows up in the process.

---

[5]Ibid., 18.
[6]Shakespeare, *Much Ado about Nothing*, 4.1.20.
[7]*Men and Marriage*, 18.

The Power of Purity

Sisters, there is power in waiting. If you give away this God-endowed power and simply act, as the apostle Paul said, "like the Gentiles who do not know God" (1 Thessalonians 4:5) and satisfy his lusts, you undermine God's work of maturing manhood. So part company with the crowd. Become a nonconformist. Swim upstream. Those who go with the flow in this matter are more likely to get the flotsam floating down the current. There are potentially good men in the mix, but how will you know the seemingly mature predatory male from the immature provider-protector type of man who is ready to grow up? Purity is the litmus test. Waiting will reveal the heart of the matter.

The simple think of their bodies as so many wood chips for building a fire. More often than not, they get burned. Simple women end up sacrificing the best years of their fertile lives on men who will *never* make themselves ready for marriage. Why? Because such women only *wish* rather than *require* that the man in their lives will marry. They hope for marriage with their "partner" when instead, if they followed God's will in this matter, they could be planning for it.

If they get pregnant during this process, outside the child-friendly confines of marriage, these women feel pressured to sacrifice their children at the Temple of Feminism—Planned Parenthood's "abortuaries." This is the world of vacuumed wombs, silent nurseries, musical beds, ringless fingers, and deep-seated rebellion against God's good and pleasing will.

The Roar of Godliness

In light of this, I have always been struck by the irony of the feminist anthem, Helen Reddy's "I Am Woman." She sings, "I am woman, hear me roar!" and continues,

> I am woman watch me grow
> See me standing toe to toe

As I spread my lovin' arms across the land
But I'm still an embryo
With a long long way to go
Until I make my brother understand.[8]

There is no doubt she means to assert the inherent dignity of women—"to make her brother understand." Yet, in throwing off modesty and chastity, what men hear being said is "use me as you will." Where's the dignity in that? The truth is that the loudest roar a woman can make, as far as making the brothers understand, is the quiet, confident restraint of choosing to be chaste till marriage. This resolve proclaims a woman's inner strength, dignity, and worth with unmistakable force and clarity.

As for brothers and how they work as they wait, and how they, too, practice sexual purity, I will address that in another context. Here I say, sisters, doing things right in matters of the heart means understanding this incredible power you wield in deciding to wait for sexual intimacy till marriage. As the subsequent chapters will show, it is this decision more than any other that will detect for you the good and godly man. As planting paperwhite narcissus and hyacinth bulbs in rocks and water in winter, this forces the best in manhood to come forth and bloom.

---

[8]Helen Reddy and Ray Burton, "I am Woman," Capitol Records, 1972.

Chapter Nine

He Protects . . . She Welcomes Protection

Women and children First!
THE MEN ON THE TITANIC

Likewise, husbands, live with your wives in an understanding way, showing honor to the woman as the weaker vessel.
1 PETER 3:7

*I*magine that I heard a door jam crack. An intruder has entered my home. My three children are asleep in their beds. My wife lies next to me. I turn to her and shake her awake. "Hey babe, there is someone in the house! I got up last time, so now it is your turn."

If equality (rather than unity) were the hallmark of our relationship, that is what I would have to say. If there is nothing distinctive in my role as a man, if we are the same and interchangeable so that equality is the issue, then we would have to make sure we share in equal measure things like confronting intruders. If I did approach it this way, my wife would not be happy. She doesn't want our equality as human beings to eradicate my distinctive role as a man. She wants me to bear a sense of responsibility to protect her.

Does this mean that she lacks the courage or strength to protect me or her children? I am quite confident that she would jump up to help me, perhaps rushing to get the kids or calling the police and praying for me as I headed down the stairs. But she would expect me to lead. In this I think she is typical, not extraordinary. *Most* women want and expect this. It is right for them to do so. Mature manhood carries a sense of protecting women and children.

Do You Smell Smoke?

Suppose there is a fire—do women really think it makes no difference who is the last one to scurry out the window? Do wives really practice egalitarianism in such moments? "We are equal, so it's simply a first-come, first-out situation. If he gets to the window first, I want him to go first. We'll have no gender-biased fire-escaping around here!" Women don't think like this. Women are honored by men who look at them as the weaker sex and therefore help them and serve them first.

When the house is on fire, it's "women and children first." The man who lives that creed will get smothering hugs and tear-drenched kisses when he finally climbs out. What do you think the husband who practices egalitarianism can expect? He stands outside the house. He watches his wife crawl out the window. What does he say? "Glad you made it out too!" Their relationship will never be the same because something profoundly disturbing has been revealed.

The Weaker Vessel

Doing things right in matters of the heart means that men want to take the lead in protecting the health and well-being of women and children. And it means that women expect this and respect men for it.

This sense of male protection is fostered in the much maligned and misunderstood passage, 1 Peter 3:7:

> Husbands, live with your wives in an understanding way, showing honor to the woman as *the weaker vessel,* since they are heirs with you of the grace of life, so that your prayers may not be hindered.

Taken out of context, the idea of women as the weaker vessel is offensive. It can be used and has been used to limit opportunities for women. But taken in context, men are being taught here to think of their wives as better by showing them honor, and weaker by providing them strength. The aim of this passage is the enhancement of womanhood by means of godly manhood. In this my wife can find no offense.

Objectively, as we have shown already, men and women are different in their strengths and weaknesses. In the economy of creation, most men are larger and stronger than women. Therefore, they have advantages that should be employed to protect and serve women in appropriate ways, beginning with their wives. When men view women as equals in strength, they are inclined to compete against them and strive to defeat them. What woman is better off as a result?

Why Darlene Became Daryl

The innateness of a man's predisposition to protect women was evidenced in a somewhat surprising fashion in the toy industry. *Newsweek* magazine reported on what those in the business call the "crash 'n' bash" theory: "Give a six year old boy a toy car and he's guaranteed to smash it against a wall or careen it off his little sister's bunk bed."[1]

The Tyco Toy Company suspected they had a winner when they took this theory directly to market with a toy car designed specifically to be crashed and bashed. They designed a plastic car

---

[1]"Feel Like a Wreck?" *Newsweek* magazine (December 14, 1992), 56.

with a crash dummy. They modeled it after the Department of Transportation (DOT) test cars, shown in commercials that depict unsecured bodies flying around on impact. Tyco made the toy car so that "on impact, the car's fenders crumple and its wheels pop off. But even more irresistible: when the plastic mini-mannequins are left unbelted, their heads and limbs go flying."

When Tyco tested the product with a group of six-year-olds, the kids went crazy with glee. A financial winner for the Tyco Company was born—just in time to become a Christmas holiday hit. However, there was one wrinkle in the concept. *Newsweek* reported, "In focus-group sessions, the company found that the DOT's female character, Darlene, didn't play well with the boys, who cringed at the notion of cracking up a girl."

Really? We can certainly train those boys to become egalitarians and stop cringing at cracking up a girl. But perhaps women are better served if we let the "boys be boys" by nurturing this natural cringe factor when girls' heads and limbs go flying off. Maybe something whole and good is at work in the male predisposition to protect women.

Tyco chose to honor the cringe factor. The crash dummy, *Darlene*, was quietly renamed *Daryl*. "He still has a strangely shaped chest," the toy company reported. But the boys were evidently not so focused on that.

The Titanic Today

When the Titanic sank, the manly call went out: "Women and children first!" Were the women demanding that 50 percent of all the seats be taken up by men? No. They understood and supported the deeper responsibilities men bear to give up their lives, if need be, to protect women and children. They were honored by it—grieved beyond words, no doubt, but honored still. Would the same thing happen today or was all that just a reflection of the times?

In 1988, *Glamour* magazine reported that 66 percent of respondents thought that if the Titanic incident were ever to be repeated, 50 percent of the seats should be reserved for men and 50 percent for women. My suspicion is that this is one of those situations in which ideology is again trying to beat down a stubborn truth. And if someone on the new Titanic ordered things that way, my suspicion is that the women sitting on those rafts would think low of the men sitting there. Women do not like egalitarianism; they are better than that. And the men who survived would have "some 'splainin' to do."[2] They would be considered weak men for not thinking of themselves as stronger and thus serving women as the weaker vessel.

My sense is that if the Titanic truly were to repeat itself, the deepest callings of manhood would surface again and the shout would go out, "Women and children first!" And the women, weeping and grieving at the impending separation, would nonetheless understand it, receive it, and be eternally honored by the sacrifice of these sexist men.

Practicing Protection

We do not face intruders, fire, crashes, and drowning on a regular basis. So let me close this chapter with a few mundane examples where manly protection expresses itself on a day-to-day basis.

Protection can be practiced in how a man walks down the street with a woman. A man who bears a strong sense to protect women will consciously walk on the curbside of the sidewalk, or, if walking on the road, on the inside walking line nearest to the oncoming traffic. Subtle, but a gesture not without meaning, and one that women are sensitive to.

A man will normally allow a woman to go first through a door. But when women are entering into a dark house or a strange room, men with a strong sense of protection will reverse course and enter first, find the lights, and check things out.

Some men wear a seatbelt more out of a desire to be safe for their wife and kids than for the obvious safety to themselves. Some

---

[2]The phrase comes from Ricky Ricardo. It was his way of getting an explanation for the various jams in which Lucy would find herself.

men like to take the lead in driving for the same reason. They feel more able to protect from behind the wheel than when riding passenger-side.

My in-laws are eighty-five years old. My mother-in-law has better stamina than my father-in-law, and so she does much more driving these days. Yet it is interesting how she always signals his leadership in this matter. She asks, "Do you want me to drive?" He makes the call. If the drive is short or he feels good, he drives. If he is unsure, he asks, "Why don't you do the driving?" In this dialog, he retains his protection over her, and she signals her glad respect for it. It has served her well through the years.

Chapter Ten

He Abstains to Protect . . . She, to Test

Suit the action to the word, the word to the action; with this special observance, that you o'erstep not the modesty of nature.

SHAKESPEARE

Treat . . . younger women as sisters, in all purity.

1 TIMOTHY 5:1–2

*I*n doing things right in matters of the heart, we now come to a development that grows from the two preceding matters: a man's responsibility to protect women and a man's equal calling to sexual purity.

The Will of God

Sexual purity is God's will for all, though mastering it, from all the evidence, is much harder for men than women. We have reason enough to pursue purity as a matter of childlike obedience to God's command.

> For this is the will of God, your sanctification: that you abstain from sexual immorality; that each one of you know how to control his own body in holiness and honor, not in the passion of lust like the Gentiles who do not know God; that no one transgress and wrong his brother in this matter, because the Lord is an avenger in all these things, as we told you beforehand and solemnly warned you. For God has not called us for impurity, but in holiness. Therefore whoever disregards this, disregards not man but God, who gives his Holy Spirit to you (1 Thessalonians 4:3–8).

What we are by gender, impulse, compulsion, or circumstance may well define the intensity of the battle we face. It does not make the battle optional; it only makes preparing for it crucial. That is what Paul is saying here in this passage. We must each know how to control ourselves "in holiness and honor, not in the passion of lust like the Gentiles who do not know God."

The moment a thief is converted and awakens to God, he knows he has to change his occupation. He can't act like he did before, when he was dead toward God. He knows this right away, because stealing was always something he understood to be wrong, but he just didn't care. His conversion is precisely a change in desire. He now cares about what pleases God, and, therefore, he immediately considers how best to earn his living.

In the same way, our outlook on sexuality will change upon conversion. Sexual sins always stain the conscience. If we continue in them, we develop a hardened or "seared conscience" (1 Timothy 4:2). But when we come to "know God," we know his will and pleasure regarding sexual purity. We can no longer follow sexual lusts as we did when we did not know God.

The apostle Paul adds more to his argument: "that no one transgress and wrong his brother in this matter" (1 Thessalonians 4:6). Sexual sins are particularly damaging to others. They are not private sins. The partner involved is profoundly affected by it, and his or her future husband or wife is injured by it.

Is the temptation and impulse strong? No doubt. Perhaps that is why Paul's word here is so direct, is repeated, and ends with such a strong warning: "Whoever disregards this, disregards not man but God, who gives his Holy Spirit to you" (v. 8).

Brothers, sexual impurity has no place for those who are in Christ. The same grace that taught you initially about God's forgiveness also trains you now to live under the influence of the Holy Spirit. "For the grace of God has appeared, bringing salvation for all people, training us to renounce ungodliness and *worldly passions*, and to live self-controlled, upright, and godly lives in the present age" (Titus 2:11–12).

Abstaining for Different Reasons

Therefore, in the outworking of sexual purity toward one another there is a complementary motive. Men protect women by their chastity. Women, by their chastity, test the maturity and character of the man pursuing them.

Another hint of this comes from 1 Timothy 5:2. "Treat . . . younger women like sisters, in all purity." For men, this is a call to mature manhood. God is fanning into flame our innate calling to protect women—in this case, from ourselves. Treat them with all the care and caution with which you would naturally defend and protect your own sister. Paul is mustering in men their self-control by tying it to their natural predisposition to protect women from injury.

Brothers, our power to abstain from sexual impurity and to practice sexual self-control with those with whom we fall in love comes from two sources. One is the love of God accompanied by a childlike desire to please him. The other is love for others, accompanied by the desire to protect, that such love prompts within us. Brothers, practice sexual self-control out of a desire to protect her from sin, guilt, shame, embarrassment, pregnancy, and the fallout that all women bear so disproportionately from sex outside of marriage.

Manhood Test Kit

Sisters, abstaining from sexual immorality is, for you, too, a matter of submitting to God and his commands. But it is more. It is God's "Mature Manhood Test Kit" for women. The immature, self-centered, ungodly man will test negative in a matter of weeks. The deceitful and cunning predator will test negative in a matter of days. Men willing to wait, and wanting to wait, will test positive. It is not a lack of sexual interest; it is a healthy fear of God. It is love, which at this point rightfully expresses itself as protection from sin and shame. If he weakens, help him succeed. If all else goes well in the development of the relationship, you know you are marrying a godly man, one who has self-control and a clear sense of his calling as a man.

Brothers, sexual purity is also a good self-test for mature manhood. Make it a top priority in the relationship. Make it a matter of your leadership. You will see yourself growing in the grace of God. As Paul said about the disciplines of the Christian life, "Practice these things, devote yourself to them, so that *all* may see your progress" (1 Timothy 4:15).

Then if all goes well in the relationship, you will be learning to lead well. If, in the unfolding of the relationship, it becomes clear that she is not the one, you have done the honorable thing. You have followed the first law of medicine contained in the Hippocratic Oath: "I will . . . never do harm to anyone." Your self-control has protected a sister in Christ, who will probably go on to be someone else's wife. She, and *he*, will deeply appreciate your manly leadership in this delicate matter of intimacy.

Chapter eleven

His Unmet Desire Drives Him toward Marriage . . . Hers Is Rewarded with Marriage

If it is harder to drag men to the altar today than it used to be, one reason is that they don't have to stop there on the way to the bedroom.

ROBERT WRIGHT

It is better to marry than to be aflame with passion.

1 CORINTHIANS 7: 9 (NIV)

I got married at age twenty-two, a little over two months short of my twenty-third birthday. I did not see it coming. Indeed on my twenty-first birthday, nothing—and I mean nothing—seemed more improbable.

Driving in an Unexpected Direction

I was a lowly college student. I was so poor that at one point I designed a way to live on fifty cents a day. The school cafeteria offered bread for five cents per slice. The peanut butter and jelly was free. I bought four slices and had two PB&J's for lunch—total: 20¢. At the grocery store I found a sale, five cans of Noodle-Os for a dollar or 20¢ per can. For dinner I bought two more slices (10¢) and heated up a can of the little spaghetti rings. Total for the day? 50¢! Yet a little over a year later, there I stood, proud and pleased on June 10, 1978, telling myself, "God has blessed you boy! God has blessed you," as my bride came walking down the aisle.

How did this happen? I met Kristen and fell in love. Just as shocking, she reciprocated. Having fallen in love, I found myself needing to protect her from myself! That got old very fast. What to do?

I arranged to be with her in more public places, often in group settings. I found myself steering her to places where we could be alone, and having gotten her there, I had to steer her out. This was an intolerable lifestyle.

I could think of only one solution—get married. I got married because I was not interested in being a virgin and leading an abstinent lifestyle. Like Billy Crystal's character Harry Burns says in the film, *When Harry Met Sally*, "When you realize you want to spend the rest of your life with somebody, you want the rest of your life to start as soon as possible."[1]

Did I worry about not having money and not being finished with school and wondering how it would all work out? Sure. But I also worried about my passions and the call to live "self-controlled, upright, and godly lives," (Titus 2:12).

Self-control is weakened by love. This word gets harder and harder to hear when your passions grow hotter and hotter. However, this is not the *only* word we have for this occasion.

---

[1] Billy Crystal character, Harry Burns, in the film *When Harry Met Sally* (1989).

Drive This Way!

First Corinthians 7: 9 says, "It is better to marry than to be aflame with passion (NIV)." Now that is a stunning word to a young man in love. It was better, I reasoned at the time, for me to get married than to continue in the pitiful state that I was then living in, no matter what loose ends there were. So I got married.

My point, and that of the apostle Paul, is that unmet sexual desire is the means by which God takes a young man who hasn't given two minutes of his whole life to think about marriage and prompts him to consider it, prepare for it, and then take the plunge.

Unmet sexual passion is like carrots: it helps a man see better what he really wants in life. Unmet sexual passion brings into focus a vision for being a husband and potentially a father. Unmet sexual passion drives him toward removing all the obstacles, whether they are inner fears and doubts or the need to work toward preparing him to know her family, to talk about their future, and to finish up what needs to be done in order to be able to make a living. It drives us to solve problems and get ready. It matures us.

The Reward of Waiting

For women, waiting is their reward. They find a good man by waiting. They are rewarded for waiting a short time when later they don't wait endlessly for him to work out all his stuff. The internal pressure prompts him to move forward. I got married at twenty-two instead of twenty-five or thirty or thirty-five, in part because of that internal pressure. My wife, who knew what she wanted and was not nearly so shocked by it all, waited patiently for me to catch up. The reward of doing things right in matters of the heart is marriage sooner rather than later.

Sisters, by waiting, your reward is also marriage to a good man. He, too, has done things right. His strength of character, his love for God, and his strong sense of protection will all carry over.

Finally, waiting until marriage to engage in sexual activity is rewarded with greater intimacy. The bonds of marriage to a good man free all restraint. Covenanted intimacy unleashes passion with no admixture of shame and guilt.

"The man and his wife were both naked and were not ashamed" (Genesis 2:25). This is free love. This is liberation. You are husband and wife together, naked. Sisters, here is your cue to speak up!

> I'll be a park, and thou shalt be my deer;
> Feed where thou wilt, on mountain, or in dale:
> Graze on my lips, and if those hills be dry,
> Stray lower, where the pleasant fountains lie.[2]

Your reward is that of the lovers in Song of Solomon. Having done things right, it was all feasting on love, the woman resting in her lover and not getting up until she pleased!

> His left hand is under my head,
> and his right hand embraces me!
> I adjure you, O daughters of Jerusalem,
> by the gazelles or the does of the field,
> that you not stir up or awaken love
> until it pleases. (Song of Solomon 2:6–7)

Running without the Restrictor Plate

Brothers, if self-control grows harder in the presence of a woman whom you love, the answer is not to set aside God's will; the answer is to set aside your qualms about marriage and get to it.

Can you make it work? Yes. If you do things right in setting up the relationship, you won't have much to change in the marriage. The cynic has said, "Servant in love, lord in marriage,"[3] suggesting men sink into lazy, demanding brutes once they are married. No doubt this happens. But it doesn't have to happen. In marriage, you

---

[2]Shakespeare, *Venus and Adonis*, 1.229.
[3]"The Franklin's Tale," *The Canterbury Tales*.

simply keep developing what you have started. Only now you run, to use a NASCAR term, without a restrictor plate.

And keep the engagement period short (three to six months). I was engaged for nine months. Too long. It was like waiting at a light that did not really look red (we were engaged, after all) or truly green (yet we weren't married). This muddied middle, interminably long in our culture, is hard on virtue and honor. The day's end—when you have studied or worked hard and then dined together, when it's nearly zero outside and you have to scrape the windshield and drive her home—is your cue. It is time to get married. Marriage is a dramatic improvement over driving her home in the cold.

A Disturbing Gift

Unmet sexual desire is a gift, a disturbing gift, but nevertheless a gift. Receive it well, and until the day comes when it is time to set it aside for the better gift, use the time to make sure that when it comes, you have already set in place the marks of a healthy, tender, passionate, enduring, mutually fulfilling relationship.

Chapter Twelve

He Displays Integrity . . . She, Inner Beauty

To me, fair friend, you never can be old,
For as you were when first your eye I ey'd,
Such seems your beauty still.

SHAKESPEARE

Train yourself for godliness; for while bodily training
is of some value, godliness is of value in every way,
as it holds promise for the present life and also for
the life to come.

1 TIMOTHY 4:7–8

*G*odliness is God's moral beauty or excellence reflected in us. God's moral excellence is a wonder to behold. "One thing have I asked of the LORD, that will I seek after: that I may dwell in the house of the LORD all the days of my life, to gaze upon the *beauty* of the LORD and to inquire in his temple" (Psalm 27:4). Godliness is also sweet to see in one another. It is moral handsomeness and creates an inner beauty in women.

To hunger for righteousness, to enjoy showing mercy, to hold preciously things like keeping your word or dealing with people in an honest and straightforward way—these are things that adorn the inner man and woman. They reflect a moral beauty that is nothing less than God at work in us, the fruit of which is godliness.

Doing things right in matters of the heart means bringing to the relationship that which lasts far longer than physical attractiveness or a profession-based income. It means showing integrity and displaying an inner beauty. It also means witnessing it in the one you give your heart to so that you are united in the values around which you are going to build your life together. Does he or she prize the basics of right and wrong, honor and respect, love for God and neighbor?

These are the right questions to ask during the formative stages of a relationship. It will not do to ask simply, "Are you a Christian?" Doing things right means looking for the character of Christ at work in that possible spouse and finding it *before* you give your heart away.

Training for Godliness

Brothers, we must prize godliness and develop our moral muscles through regular exercise. Paul writes, "*Train* yourself for godliness; for while bodily training is of some value, godliness is of value in every way, as it holds promise for the present life and also for the life to come" (1 Timothy 4:7–8). Pump iron if you wish, but pump integrity more. "Whoever walks in integrity walks securely, but he who makes his ways crooked will be found out" (Proverbs 10:9).

Brothers, in making a deal and honoring it, in turning your eye from suggestive pictures, in not cheating on an exam no matter how important passing it is for your career plans, in telling the truth as it is (humble as it may be) on your resume, in meeting your obligations, in cherishing honesty and in practicing humility, in admitting your errors and owning up to your faults—in all these your moral muscles get a workout.

Besides building muscles, physical training is also about heart rate. We've got to put time into running those miles, or swimming those laps, or riding that bike. Whatever gets the heart rate going for twenty or thirty minutes several times a week will do. A similar routine will work for training in godliness. Get your heart before God, and get your heart racing to know him and to be excited about what he is doing in the world and your part in it. Trace out the sovereign history of God's redemption by reading the Bible— Genesis to Revelation. Memorize key portions of Scripture. Read about those who "expect great things from God and attempt great things for God"[1] Praise him in the sanctuary. Start tithing and give generously to things that save lives and change lives. These things will get you past minimalist Christianity, out of the baby pool and into the ocean.

Imperishable Beauty

Sisters, if the only charm you have is your physical appearance, beautiful as you may be, you are foolish and will come to rue the day you scoffed at the value of inner beauty. You will find a man for whom physical beauty is also the main thing. What then happens as you age? You will grow more insecure with every birthday. In vain you will subject yourself to chasing cosmetics like a dog chasing a meat wagon. You will become one of the empty, frighteningly sad women who submit to face lifts, breast surgery, and Botox injections (if you escape the deadly grip of anorexia). By midlife, you will be popping antidepressants.

Remember the proverb, "Charm is deceitful, and beauty is vain, but a woman who fears the LORD is to be praised" (Proverbs 31:30). When it comes to appearance, Tallulah Bankhead's (1903–1968) axiom is worth remembering: "There is less here than meets the eye." Instead, "Let your adorning be the hidden person of the heart with the *imperishable beauty* of a gentle and quiet spirit,

---

[1]This phrase was coined by the great missionary William Carey. If you want a thrilling read about his experiences, I recommend Vishal and Ruth Mangalwadi, *The Legacy of William Carey: A Model for the Transformation of a Culture* (Wheaton, IL: Crossway, 1994).

which in God's sight is very precious" (1 Peter 3:4). The brothers also find it of great worth.

The Body Project

The Body Project is a study by Joan Jacobs Brumberg of girls' diaries. In one diary from around 1890, a young girl scribbled her New Year's resolutions: "Resolved: to think before speaking. To work seriously. To be self-restrained in conversation and actions. Not to let my thoughts wander. To be dignified. Interest myself more in others." Brumberg writes that this was typical of the times. In 1990 a typical entry went, "I will try to make myself better in any way I possibly can . . . I will lose weight, get new lenses, already got a new haircut, good makeup, new clothes and accessories."[2]

Could the differences be clearer? One focused entirely on improving her life, the other merely on her looks.

Physical beauty is of some value, as we noted in 1 Timothy 4:8. All men know what Shakespeare meant when he said,

> Where is any author in the world
> teaches such beauty as a woman's eye?[3]

And that is just the eye! But sisters, the man who will make for you a healthy, tender, passionate, enduring, mutually fulfilling life partner is a man who prizes faith and integrity in himself and goes weak in the knees at your inner beauty too. This beauty ages well—it is an "imperishable beauty." It is this beauty that men see and appreciate as you grow through the seasons of life.

> To me, fair friend, you never can be old,
> For as you were when first your eye I ey'd,
> Such seems your beauty still.[4]

---

[2] *A Return to Modesty*, 142.
[3] Shakespeare, *Love's Labour's Lost*, 4.3.312.
[4] Shakespeare, *Sonnets*, 104.1.

Friendship, faithfulness, generosity of spirit, godliness—these traits grow more beautiful to behold over time. A good man will have a keen eye for them. A godly man will cherish them. He may not find the word to express it, but the English poet Robert Browning (1812–1889) said it well-enough for us all:

Grow old along with me!
The best is yet to be,
The last of life, for which the first was made.
Our times are in his hand.[5]

[5]Robert Browning, "Rabbi Ben Ezra," St. 1.

Chapter Thirteen

He Loves by Sacrificing . . .
She, by Submitting

Harry: There are two kinds of women;
high maintenance and low maintenance.
Sally: Which one am I?
Harry: You're the worst kind. You're high maintenance
but you think you're low maintenance.
WHEN HARRY MET SALLY

Faith, hope and love abide, these three;
but the greatest of these is love.
1 CORINTHIANS 13:13

*D*oing things right in matters of the heart means, of course, loving well over the long haul. In the interplay of male sacrifice and female submission, we are very near the visible out-working of love itself. We are practically on holy ground, and given that this matter reflects the very essence of our union with Christ, it may be holy ground indeed.

War and Peace

The "third rail" in discussing matters of the heart is submission: "Wives, *submit* to your own husbands, as to the Lord" (Ephesians 5:22). These are "fightin' words" in the long war between the sexes. Before I weigh in, I would first like to make the situation worse by pointing out that we are also at war with ourselves (Romans 7:21–25). Our Spirit, agreeing with the Word of God, desires to do the right thing, but our flesh, fiercely contesting our conversion, asserts selfishness and pride in a hundred skirmishes a day. In a sense, when two people strive to become one, four desires are striving to become one. To this we add the inevitable conflict that arises from joining two people with different personalities and vastly different life-shaping experiences—*and* the fact that one is male and the other is female—and no wonder the establishment of a healthy, tender, passionate, enduring, mutually fulfilling relationship is held up to so much ridicule. We never quite sync up, and we never will. It appears to me this all comes to a head precisely at this point, on the matter of submission.

It is supercharged by our personality type and understood according to how it filters through our life experiences. It is railed against by our rebellious flesh and yet is declared by the Spirit with confident simplicity to be the right way to go. Let God be true and every man a liar.

You First

Let's begin by returning to the heart of the matter. The goal of marriage is unity, two becoming one. Disunity is the way of all things because of our fallen nature. To buck the trend, to reverse the way of all flesh, to equip us for the battle for oneness of spirit in a life shared together, God teaches us some holy manners. God calls the man to love by sacrificing his immediate desires for those of her overall well-being and happiness. He calls the woman to submit her more immediate desires to his overall well-being and happiness. They are like two people running to get out of the rain and arriving together at the door. "You first." "No, *you* first."

Where to Dinner, Dear?

It may appear as a trifle, but it is not. At this stage in our lives, with kids grown and gone and our energy levels a bit in decline, when we are tired and have stuff to talk over, we stop somewhere for dinner. I get behind the wheel and ask, "Where to dinner, dear?" I ask because it will make me happy to go somewhere that will please her.

She replies, "Whereever you want is fine." She says this because she is happy to go somewhere that I might have a hankering for, and she is pleased when I am pleased.

I return, "What I *want* is to go to the place that would make you the happiest to go, wherever that is, within a one-thousand-mile radius of this car!" I say this now to amplify my motive in asking her in the first place.

She responds, "Well, John E., if you *really* want to make me happy, I would like you to choose, for *that* will make me happy."

We are at a stalemate of sorts, two people bowing to the other and clunking heads. So I say, "Well if I *had* to choose what I want, I guess I would try that Peking Palace Buffet."

She looks a bit chagrined. "Well . . . when I said, 'You choose,' I forgot to add, 'anywhere but Chinese food.' I can't eat that food at this time of night. How about that barbeque place?"

To that I reply, "That would be good, but when I said within one thousand miles, I really meant no more than five miles. That barbeque place is thirty minutes away in this traffic and I would have to get more gas, which means we would have to turn around and go back the other way or pay premium prices. I don't want to do that." We are stalemated again. It has been revealed that we do indeed have our own private desires that don't naturally match up.

Being the leader, it is time for me to offer a way forward. "How about that family restaurant by the school?"

"Yes, that will be fine," she demurs. I do not detect enough energy in her tone of voice to bolster my confidence. But off I go. I think of the chicken parmesan I had there once and start looking forward to it. I know she will enjoy something similar. On the way, I spot a Panera Bread restaurant. It's not my favorite. But I remember how much Kristen likes things like strawberry and walnut salads and hot panini turkey sandwiches on rosemary focaccia bread. I swerve in. Goodbye, chicken parm, hello, chicken soup. I see her smile at me. Victory!

Love Bows

Now if you think this all a bit of silliness, talk to a family law attorney. These attorneys will tell you that in the final days of a dying marriage, they watch with painful embarrassment as two people fight over wastebaskets. Every decision has become a contest of wills, from big to small to petty. Each is another skirmish in the larger battle that rages between them. Both people now fight hard for what they want, at the expense of the other.

Their love is on its deathbed. But the mortal blow was struck when they first moved from seeking their happiness in the well-being and joy of the other to seeking it independently from the other. Fights over Tupperware are just the final blows in the murder of covenantal love.

The dilemma my wife and I face in where to dine is rooted in the very significant and life-giving principle of seeking our own happiness in the happiness of the other. This, you may note, is the title of the next chapter. The two are inseparably woven together. In practice, it gets a little awkward at times, and much more so when you truly do have a strong desire or opinion seeking to be satisfied, and the other does too. Since this is the stuff of common conflict that every couple must confront, it only underscores the importance of the two matters now before us, here and in the next chapter.

What Happens When You Say, "I Don't Believe in Fairies"?

Sacrificing and submitting must become the established patterns of our lives, especially in seeking agreement and resolution (remember: unity—not winning—is the heart of the matter) when the inevitable conflicts come. Without unity as the goal, battles are won and lost in daily interchanges of "what about what I want?" and "what about my needs?" Whenever these words are spoken, something in the relationship dies. Uttering these words is the equivalent of saying "I don't believe in fairies!" while in Neverland. These words kill. Unity has been sacrificed on the altar of self. One has returned to two. It is no longer "you and me against the world!" It has become "to each his own."

God has provided a way forward. As we sacrifice and submit, God is equipping us for the battle against our inherent selfishness as two individual sinful people. It is the right thing to do. It promotes the unity of spirit essential to a healthy, tender, passionate, enduring, mutually fulfilling life together.

Love Sacrifices and Submits

The complementary call to manly sacrifice and womanly submission comes from Ephesians 5:15–33. There are specific directives here regarding matters of the heart that grow out of general directives about living wisely in this sinful world.

> Look *carefully* then how you walk, not as unwise but as wise, making the best use of the time, because the days are evil. Therefore do not be foolish, but understand what the will of the Lord is. And do not get drunk with wine, for that is debauchery, but be *filled with the Spirit*, addressing one another in psalms and hymns and spiritual songs, singing and making melody to the Lord with your heart, giving thanks always and for everything to God the Father in the name of our Lord Jesus Christ, *submitting* to one another out of reverence for Christ. (5:15–21)

In a real sense, husbands and wives are equally called to submit to each other. We are all "living as servants of God" (1 Peter 2:16) in all our relationships. This I take to be the meaning of Paul's words in Ephesians 5:21: "submitting to *one another* out of reverence for Christ." In matters of the heart, we are expressing this equality of submission when we say, "Your wish is my command." It is not given as a command, but it is taken as such because love loves to express itself as service.

There is also a complementary way we submit to one another. In a marriage of two equals, the way a husband shows his reverent submission to Christ is in submitting to the burden of leadership. The way a wife shows her reverent submission to Christ is in respecting her husband's obligation to lead and submitting to it in spite of his weakness and inadequacies. So, we read:

> Wives, submit to your own husbands, as to the Lord. For the husband is the head of the wife even as Christ is the head of the church, his body, and is himself its Savior. Now as the church submits to Christ, so also wives should submit in everything to their husbands. (Ephesians 5:22–24)

The reason we are not put off (or should not be put off) by the words, "submit in everything," is because, as we have already shown, this is a general disposition of the heart. We know this because when Paul summarizes his meaning, he puts it specifically in the language of attitude: "Let the wife see that she *respects* her husband" (5:33). Submission is a disposition or attitude of honor and respect for her husband as the leader.

Hypotheticals Don't Bite

If I asked Kristen to sell marijuana in the park to boost our flagging book sale income, she would not do it. It's never right to do wrong (see 1 Samuel 25:14–19; Acts 5:29). Her general disposition to obey the laws of the land and her obedience to the law of neighborly love would restrain her. To the degree that there is no conflict between God's *holiness* and her husband's *happiness*, she will respect and support me as best she can. And if she had to say no to something, she would still do so out of a heart (a disposition) that longs to support me. She would say something like, "John E., you don't mean that. You're just worried." And being a helpmate she might add, "Perhaps we can move to a smaller house or together write a better book."

This story is not completely fictitious. A woman in my church— a mother with three children—once came to me for help because her husband was planning to sell marijuana out of her home. Such situations are heart-wrenching and difficult to sort out. Yet for most people, this is more hypothetical than real-life experience. And hypotheticals don't bite. The apostles knew the limits of obeying any man (Acts 5:29), yet since Paul doesn't mention this in Ephesians 5:22–24, I take it to mean that here he is addressing the day-to-day, routine, normal experiences of life.

In general, good men are not trying to do wrong, even when they make many mistakes. Johnny Cash, for example, struggled much of his life with alcohol and amphetamines, and over the years felt God had to wear him down before he could be lifted up. He wrote of his struggles in *The Man in Black*, describing these inner demons. He was never an easy man to be married to. Yet his wife, June, wrote,

> I choose to be Mrs. Johnny Cash in my life. I decided I'd allow him to be Moses, and I'd be Moses' brother Aaron, picking his arms up and padding along behind him. I stayed in submission to my husband, and he allowed me to do anything I wanted to. I felt like I was lucky to have that kind of romance."[1]

We may acknowledge the limitations of this call, but let's be honest. Sisters, it is hard for you to submit, period, even to a good man, in anything. It is submission itself that riles you. Don't hide

---

[1] June Carter, *Ring of Fire: A Tribute to Johnny Cash* (Nashville, TN: Rutledge Hill, 2003), 50.

behind a hypothetical situation. Submission is the way of life and love in matters of the heart.

I will add by way of encouragement that submission is simply not that hard on a day-to-day basis. My wife could tell a few stories where it was a struggle, but those incidents occurred over the course of thirty years! She would tell you that it has been far more a delight and a relief than ever it was a burden.

If you do things right in searching out and constructing a good and healthy relationship, filtering out the self-centered and immature and finding in your man the basic provider-protector, you will have a similar experience. If he knows what it means to be a man and demonstrates a servant leadership through the early and formative stages of the relationship, you will want him to go on leading that way. You will naturally be pulling for him. You will submit to his best judgment because, though by no means faultless, he is a man who loves God and loves you. Set aside your fear and exercise faith in this matter.

Hey, Where Are You Going?

Brothers, as husbands (or future ones), our love is to be expressed as *sacrifice*.

> Husbands, love your wives, as Christ loved the church and *gave himself up for her,* that he might sanctify her, having cleansed her by the washing of water with the word, so that he might present the church to himself in splendor, without spot or wrinkle or any such thing, that she might be holy and without blemish. (Ephesians 5:25–27)

Christ loved his bride, and it came through as sacrifice. Christ did not sacrifice his headship (thereby abandoning his calling); he was expressing it. Christ's supreme act of headship was to go ahead and do what was required, even sacrificing his own life, to serve his bride the church. He did not say, to put it in the creedal form of every passive husband, "Yeah, whatever." That is not sacrifice;

it is abandonment. Nor, even though he is God, did he lord it over people. He woos and wins through love and patience. Chaucer is right:

> There is one thing, sirs, that I can safely say:
> that those bound by love must obey each other
> if they are to keep company long.
> Love will not be constrained by mastery;
> When mastery comes, the god of love at once
> Beats his wings and farewell—he is gone.[2]

Our part, as men in this, is to serve and sacrifice, not swagger and sound off. The marvelous children's poet Shel Silverstein illustrates what happens if we don't:

> If you want to marry me, here's what you'll have to do:
> You must learn how to make a perfect
>   chicken-dumpling stew.
> And you must sew my holey socks,
> And soothe my troubled mind,
> And develop the knack for scratching my back,
> And keep my shoes spotlessly shined.
> And while I rest you must rake up the leaves,
> And when it is hailing and snowing
> You must shovel the walk . . . and be still when I talk.
> And—hey—where are you going?[3]

Manly love looks to sacrifice. We lay our own wants and desires down in order to serve her wants and desires. This is not an absolute but a disposition. Not all her desires are consistent with God's desires, and so we must please him above all others. But to the degree that there is no conflict between God's *holiness* and our wife's *happiness*, we are willing to make the sacrifice.

---

[2] "The Franklin's Tale," *The Canterbury Tales*, 297.
[3] Shel Silverstein, "My Rules," *Where the Sidewalk Ends* (New York: HarperCollins, 1974), 74.

Not Every Night Is Candlelight and Chardonnay

My story about asking, "Where to dinner, dear?" is significant. It reflects the general paradigm and tone of our pre-married and now long-married lives. I look to sacrifice; she looks to submit. Sometimes it is easy. Sometimes it takes time to work out. We come to every issue of our lives together with the disposition of manly sacrifice and womanly submission.

Brothers and sisters, it is important to practice and observe this in any matter involving your heart. Sisters, if you are all about serving and he is all about being served, sing, "I'm gonna wash that man right outa my hair!"[4] Brothers, if she is all demanding and manipulating to meet her black hole of emotional needs, run!

Brothers, look to sacrifice and take note when she yields to your wishes. Sisters, yield to his holy happiness and mark it well when he says, "No, I prefer we go with your idea." Marry that man!

In practice, it is easy on occasion. Wedding plans are an example. Our bride-to-be may ask us all kinds of questions about our preferences for flowers and meals and a thousand other things. Most men I know have clearer ideas about what they want to plan for after the wedding: where they will go that night, where they will honeymoon, etc. But as far as the ceremony, more often than not they offer a simple, "Whatever *pleases* you, pleases me." The same is true when it comes to the home and how it is laid out and arranged. We men are usually happy to defer. "Arrange it how you please. When you are happy, I am happy."

Other areas require real bowing towards each other. How money is spent, when it is spent, where it is spent—that takes some serious sacrificing and submitting until there is a unity of agreement. Deciding how much time we will give to work rather than to home requires, sometimes, the sacrifice of potential career

---

[4] Rodgers and Hammerstein, "I'm Gonna Wash That Man Right Outa My Hair," *South Pacific*, 1959.

advancement. At other times, it requires the wife to offer submissive support of her husband, who is driven by a deep inward need to build something or impact something in the world around him. Where to live, how big a house to buy or rent, one car or two, new or used, where you spend your holidays, what matters of ministry and mission will get your time and charity—when these are all sifted through the sieve of manly sacrifice and womanly submission, the two become one and nothing can tear it asunder. Even intimacy itself requires a little sacrifice and submission. One night it may be, "Ok, dear, I will wait till you are less tired." Another time it may be, "I was not much in the mood, but okay." Not every night is candlelight and chardonnay.

Chapter Fourteen

He Seeks His Happiness in Hers . . . She Seeks Hers in His

A good marriage is that in which each appoints
the other guardian of his solitude.

RAINER MARIA RILKE

He who loves his wife loves himself.

EPHESIANS 5:28

We turn now to develop what has already been mentioned. In matters of the heart, the right thing to do is for him to seek his happiness in making her happy, and for her to seek her happiness in making him happy.

When Is a Sacrifice Not a Sacrifice and Submission Not a Loss?

When God sets forth the complementary expression of love—manly sacrifice and womanly submission—he connects it to something so profound and powerful that it must be highlighted as its own directive in doing things right in matters of the heart. To grasp it, first grasp this: Brothers, to love sacrificially is not a sacrifice! Sisters, in submitting you are not giving up something, you are gaining something!

What do I mean? How can this be so? Let's begin with Ephesians 5:25–27:

> Husbands, love your wives, as Christ loved the church and gave himself up for her, that he might sanctify her, having cleansed her by the washing of water with the word, so that he might present the church to *himself* in splendor, without spot or wrinkle or any such thing, that she might be holy and without blemish.

Brothers, when is sacrifice not a sacrifice? When you gain by it. Christ laid down his life in order to present to himself a radiant bride! So let us be clear on this. Did Christ sacrifice? Yes, he laid down his life. He did not, however, sacrifice in the sense of loss but in the sense of gain. He lost his life to win for himself a spotless and resplendent bride.

Confirmation that we are reading this correctly is found in Hebrews 12:2. It says of Christ and the cross, "who for the *joy* set before him *endured* the cross." There is nothing joyful about the cross; it was something he endured. The strength to make the sacrifice and endure it came from the gain he saw that was to be won through it—joy. "The joy set before him" refers to the anticipated increase of joy (or holy happiness) that was to be his in the redemption of repentant sinners who would put their hope in him for the forgiveness of their sins and be forever united in him by his Spirit. Christ's sacrifice, as is true with all godly sacrifice, is a sacrifice that brings gain. Sacrifice is a means of increasing and fulfilling our own lives. Sacrificial love always increases personal joy in the long run. It is a self-fulfilling self-sacrifice.

Let's Sell This House!

My wife came to me some years ago and said she wanted to sell our house and buy another fixer-upper. I was stunned. We had worked for ten years fixing up our home. I was settled, happy, comfortable, and in no mood to pack. She was restless. She had taken this old house and made it special. I was now enjoying it. She was chomping for a new project. I started to say, "No way," but somehow it came out, "Why?"

She told me about her interests and desires, and I moaned and fussed and acted like she had just struck me with an arrow. "I love this house. I could live here another ten years easily." However, I knew then it was just a matter of *when*. It was not an ungodly proposal. It would not interfere with what we felt called to do in Boston, and I knew it would make her happy! And I know that I get joy in making her happy.

Within six months we had bought an old fixer-upper and started all over again. It took us another six years of scraping and painting; we spent one whole year remodeling a bathroom, and we had two bathrooms! We did argue about the pace of things, but in the end she had made another warm and lovely home. I sacrificed and got myself a bundle of joy in return.

Submitting Is the Way Up to Heaven

Sisters, in the same way, your submission to Christ does not result in a personal loss. It is a gain, or you would not now be following Christ. You gave way to Christ to gain a better life. You have experienced the truth of Christ's word, "Whoever finds his life will lose it, and whoever loses his life for my sake will find it" (Matthew 10:39). What is true in matters of the soul is true in matters of the heart.

Peter once tried to remind Jesus of how great a sacrifice he had made to follow him. Jesus reminded Peter that such things are not losses but gains:

"See, we have *left everything* and followed you." Jesus said, "Truly, I say to you, there is no one who has left house or brothers or sisters or mother or father or children or lands, for my sake and for the gospel, who will not receive a hundredfold now in this time, houses and brothers and sisters and mothers and children and lands, with persecutions, and in the age to come eternal life (Mark 10:28–30).

Should We Sacrifice and Submit to Gain Our Own Joy?

The joy and gain that comes by way of sacrifice and submission is not some side benefit that we are to pretend is a surprise to us, as if it were not part of our *motive* in doing so. Indeed, we are instructed to focus on it and remember it. "Bless the LORD, O my soul, and forget not all his benefits" (Psalm 103:2). In submitting, we gain Christ and his righteousness. He gains our praise.

> I will greatly rejoice in the LORD;
> my soul shall exalt in my God,
> for he has clothed me with the garments of salvation;
> he has covered me with the robe of righteousness.
>   (Isaiah 61:10)

If My Wife Is Hungry, I Have Not Yet Finished Eating

Scripture takes this same principle of sacrifice and submission as the way to joyful self-fulfillment and applies it to lovers. "In the same way," Paul says, referring to how Christ sacrificed to gain a resplendent bride for himself, husbands ought to sacrifice for their advancement of the joy in marriage.

> *In the same way* husbands should love their wives as their own bodies. He who loves his wife loves himself. For no one ever hated his own flesh, but nourishes and cherishes it, just as Christ does the church, because we are members of his body. "Therefore a man shall leave his father

and mother and hold fast to his wife, and the two shall become one flesh." This mystery is profound, and I am saying that it refers to Christ and the church. However, let each one of you love his wife as himself, and let the wife see that she respects her husband. (Ephesians 5:28–33)

The power, or motivation, for sacrificing and submitting comes from seeking your own happiness in the other person's well-being, as if your spouse is truly an extension of your own body. Sacrifice and submission are self-fulfilling.

I naturally get up in the morning and respond to my need to feel clean. So I wash up and brush my teeth. I feel a groaning within and consider breakfast. I recall my love of a great cup of coffee and go after it. I ask intuitively which will make me happier: a bagel right from the toaster, a full plate of eggs and sausage, or just the coffee? I do what makes me happiest. If I burn my finger on the toaster, I naturally run cold water on it to relieve the pain. This is what Paul is pointing to when he says, "no one ever hated his own flesh, but nourishes and cherishes it" (5:29). Our union as man and woman comes when a natural pursuit of our own well-being is extended to our spouse. My joy is completed in my wife's good. This is what it means to love our wives "as our own bodies" (5:28).

In practice, this means that if my wife is still hungry, I have not yet finished breakfast. If she is burned, I, too, think of ice and cool water. When she gets the medical care she needs and is at rest, then I can breathe a sigh of relief. It means that if she has a strong desire to do something, I want to help her fulfill it. For when she is fulfilled in her life, I am full and rich indeed. This is the very essence of love, the true heart of the matter. This is how it is that "the two shall become one flesh."

What, Then, Is Selfishness?

Love is basically seeking your own happiness in the well-being of another. It may be more than that, but it will never be less.

Selfishness, the deadly enemy of love, is not "seeking your own need." Selfishness is seeking your own need separately from the needs of others, or at the expense of others, or apart from God. This is the kind of self-seeking that is condemned (Romans 2:8). The opposite of selfishness is not selflessness. That is often the lofty language of altruistic idealism run amok. The opposite of selfishness is self-fulfillment in the holy joy and well-being of others. This is doable.

Seek your happiness in the holy happiness of the other. Sacrifice and submit to that end, and you can no more be divided than you can go out to dinner and leave your stomach at home.

Chapter Fifteen

He Is the Primary Provider for the Family . . . She, the Primary Nurturer

To business that we love we rise betime,
And go to't with delight.

SHAKESPEARE

God blessed them. And God said to them,
"Be fruitful and multiply and fill the earth and subdue it."

GENESIS 1:28

*T*he key in this matter is the word *primary*. As we noted earlier, God has ordained two spheres of human labor in his call to us to "fill the earth and subdue it" (Genesis 1:28). The first sphere points to the fruitful labor of bearing children and managing a home. The second points to the labor we bring to the external world around us. When children are added, both partners contribute to both spheres but in complementary proportions.

The father is called to labor primarily as the breadwinner for the family. The mother is primarily responsible for nurturing the family. This pattern has long proven to be an extremely economical and prosperous arrangement and one that produces healthy and productive children.

Making Bread and Buttering It

For as long as I have known, courted, married, and raised a family with my wife, Kristen, she has done things to earn income. She worked full-time while I went to seminary. Then the babies came, and I started working full-time as the breadwinner. Her primary work became the home and the raising of our children. My primary work was outside the home working as a pastor. Secondarily I gave as much time to my family as was possible. Kristen gave most of her time to the raising of our children and the management of our home. Even so, she was always looking to supplement our income.

For many years, she hosted foreign exchange students who came to Boston to study English. She earned about nine hundred dollars a month for each student who lived with us. We had students about seven months out of the year, so she earned about six thousand dollars annually for the family while managing our home and raising our three children.

For the last ten years she has had a bulk-mailing job in which she labels postcards for a local business. There have been times when the kids and I have helped as we watch a movie or a Red Sox game. But mostly she does it on her own. She earns another four thousand dollars a year for the family doing this. Along the way she also home-schooled our children for a number of years. Since we lived in the inner city of Boston, this saved our children from a poor educational experience and saved us tens of thousands of dollars in private school expenses.

Then she decided it was time to move after fixing up our fixer-upper, as I mentioned earlier. We bought a house that was in worse shape than the first house we had bought in Boston. We both saw that the new house was a solid one, and with a little *TLC* and sweat-equity it could be a lovely home. She took charge, and I followed her "honey-do" list. It took us another six years to get it in shape. By this time our children were preparing for college, so we sold the house. We made well over one hundred thousand dollars on the sale. This enabled us to help with our children's college expenses. All this my wife earned while never leaving the home. When the children left home, she went on staff at the pregnancy center, earning more funds for college. Had she had a professional degree and a particular career passion, she no doubt would have turned her attention to it at this time.

In this way she has followed the path of wise women throughout history who take pride in the management of their home, who know the infinite worth of rearing children and still finding ways to use their skills industriously and for profit.

You Go Save the World!

In all she did during that time, Kristen took to heart the admonition of Titus 2:4–5: "Train the young women to love their husbands and children, to be self-controlled, pure, *working at home*, kind, and submissive to their own husbands, that the word of God may not be reviled."

Titus 2:4–5 does not limit a mother to working only at home. It only makes the home a worthy and needy sphere of labor and calls for wives to approach it as a matter of primary importance. The thing I most resent about modernity is how it demeans what my wife chose to do, and how, in general, it teaches wives not to make their husbands, children, and home a vocation worthy of their best efforts.

We are at another juncture where nonconformity and rebellion to the times are in order. Sisters, when you get married and when you have children, turn your heart towards home and love the challenges it brings. Don't let people tell you that your worth is validated in what you do at a corporation or a courthouse or a hospital.

My wife, Kristen, once said to me, "John E., you go save the world. My mission field is these three souls." She would not be seduced into thinking that there was something better or more important or more fulfilling "out there"—not as long as her three children were "in here." She had important work to do, and she would not farm it out to daycare workers and nannies. She was the expert; they were hirelings. She didn't always feel confident about her expertise as a mother; in truth, she struggled with it much of the time. I was sure that she was better at it than she felt and that the fruit would appear in good season. And it did.

She also took a great measure of pride in knowing that whatever I was able to do in the marketplace was because of the stability she created in the home.

> Her husband is known in the gates
> when he sits among the elders of the land (Proverbs 31:23).

It is not false humility when men dedicate their books to their wives, or when men, feted at the pinnacle of their profession, point to their wives as the cause of their success. It is a simple matter of honesty.

The Inherent Dignity of Motherhood

Proverbs 31 is celebration of praise for the inherent dignity of women who make a conscious decision to love their husband and children well. It fetes the wife and mother for her own high achievement, for making her home the *primary* focus of her labor while secondarily seeking out profitable and productive outlets for her skills and talents.

The wife's primary focus is on her husband and her children. "She does [her husband] good" (31:12). "She looks well to the ways of her household" (31:27). In carrying out this labor, she is described as strong, confident, and productive. "She dresses herself with strength and makes her arms strong" (31:17).

It is noteworthy that the more our culture tells women to be "out there" and tells them not to focus too much on being "merely a wife and mother," the more women have become psychologically fragile, emotionally insecure, anorexic, and ever-searching for self-esteem in the approval of others.

Not so the woman of Proverbs 31. She dresses herself with inner strength and inner beauty. She knows who she is and is confident about what her role is and about the value of her primary labor. She makes her home the primary focus of her life and works at it with ever-improving skill. She develops an eye for quality and knows what to do with it. "She seeks wool and flax, and works with willing hands" (Proverbs 31:13). She works at meeting the needs of her family. "She rises while it is yet night and provides food for her household and portions for her maidens" (31:15).

She is also looking to supplement her family financially and applies her talents to that end. "She considers a field and buys it; with the fruit of her hands she plants a vineyard" (31:16). She sees that industriousness produces a profit. "She perceives that her merchandise is *profitable*. Her lamp does not go out at night" (31:18). After taking care of her family and profiting from her work, she is charitable. "She opens her hand to the poor and reaches out her hands to the needy" (31:20). She is not a "dumb housewife" as some disparage this calling. She is intelligent and seen as intelligent. "She opens her mouth with *wisdom*, and the teaching of kindness is on her tongue" (31:26). She works hard at it. "She looks well to the ways of her household and does not eat the bread of idleness" (31:27).

Sisters, should God, in his sovereignty, bless you with a good man and bless you with children, then be confident to swim against the current. Doing the right thing in matters of the heart means making your top priority the care of your husband, children, and home and secondarily finding things to do "out there."

Some wives do this by working one or two days a week as dental hygienists or as nurses. Others become freelance writers to give vent to their passion. Home businesses or part-time work can put your larger talents to work, especially as the children grow older. But beware: latch-key kids, children who come home after school to a parentless environment, are in serious danger. Sex, drugs, and alcohol are hunting for our youth, and the feeding hours are three to six o'clock in the afternoon. The mother who is not there to protect them is risking her children to these predators. When the kids are grown and gone, then take up your next challenge full-time if you please. Until then, make your home your primary focus for your talents and labor.

Storming the Castle

Brothers, as our wives look for extra ways to bring in income to the family, we are looking for ways to get in extra time with our families because our primary responsibility in marriage, where children are present, is to be the breadwinner. Our primary sphere of labor is in the external world. When I leave home to go off to preach and teach and do my thing, my wife says to me, "Have fun storming the castle!"[1]

Given the constant ridicule of this arrangement in the popular culture, we do well to remind ourselves that this actually is the way most women want things to be, so long as they don't feel the pressure to act or say otherwise for approval. They want the man in their life to be a good provider.

A Good-looking Stethoscope

A seventeen-year study by Syracuse University revealed that when it comes to understanding what men and women are attracted to, even today, men seek beauty and women seek providers. Anthropology professor John Townsend, a product of the liberal 1960s and author of the study, believed we would "slough off our

---

[1] The line comes from the film *The Princess Bride*, 1987.

confining, outmoded sex roles and become freer, more actualized human beings." He found women have a different view of what it is to be actualized and fulfilled human beings.

He reported, "It happened in the Bible, it happened in ancient Athens, it happened in Margaret Mead's Samoa, and it's happening here. If a man meets a woman working a lunch-counter, 'if she's beautiful, he'll date her.'" But for women, the perceived ability to provide, no matter his looks, made him attractive.[2]

Townsend further tested his results with college students, asking them who they would consider dating and marrying. He showed them various models with a range of physical characteristics from homely to good-looking. He presented them in various forms of dress from blue blazers to fast-food shirts. Townsend says he was startled by the results. Put a handsome man in a fast-food shirt and he sits home on Friday nights. Put a homely man in a blue blazer with a stethoscope around his neck and it's, "Yes, I will be glad to have dinner with you." That must be some good-looking stethoscope.

He Trains and Disciplines When Home . . . She Welcomes the Takeover

Complementing a wife's efforts to earn extra income or find outlets for some of her talents untapped in the home, a wise husband looks to be at home as much as possible. When he comes home, he takes over, he takes charge, he takes responsibility for matters of instruction and discipline. And wives are glad for the relief.

Dr. James Dobson of Focus on the Family made an interesting point, given what we have just said about the complementary priorities of a husband and wife with children. He said, "If the children are disrespectful and disobedient, the primary responsibility lies with the father . . . not his wife." Now if the primary sphere of labor for mothers is the home, why are they not primarily responsible for the outcome? The answer goes back to what we

---

[2]Laura T. Ryan, "Men Still Like Looks as Women Eye Providers," *Boston Herald* (June 3, 1999), 6.

said earlier. Men are called as husbands and fathers to be the head of their families. So Dobson says, "The Christian man is obligated to lead his family to the best of his abilities. . . . Likewise, he bears heavier responsibility for the outcome of those decisions."[3]

When I came home and took charge, my wife was glad of it. When I didn't, she was resentful. I would trudge home in the cold and snow, climb the stairs, breathe in the welcoming smells of bread and soup, find my wife, give her a kiss, tell her how weary I was, and she would say, "Yes, dear. *Your* children are waiting for you. Have at it."

When the fights broke out, when discipline was needed, it was expected that it was mine to deal with. It was my watch. When we were both home, it was mine to lead. This is the way my wife wanted it. I think most wives want it this way.

In addition, it falls to me as the man to provide a vision for our children about God and his ways and purposes for them. "Fathers . . . bring them up in the discipline and instruction of the Lord" (Ephesians 6:4). So when I am home, I lead in prayer. I lead the family to worship. I talk with them about right and wrong and wise and foolish choices. My wife does this all day long. When I come home, it's my turn.

The Dessert Portion of the Day

All children crave fatherly attention, and the wise and loving father will give it. Children think of their father as a love sponge. They simply must squeeze him and have his affection and attention run willy-nilly all over them. Children see the lesser portion of time they receive from their father as the *dessert* portion.

And in true complementary fashion, fathers tend to play differently with their kids from how mothers do, and by this means they prepare them for life in different ways. Fathers instinctively heft their babies up and play a little more roughly with them. Babies howl with delight. Fathers are more apt to wrestle and roughhouse

---

[3]James Dobson, *Straight Talk to Men and Their Wives* (Waco: TX, Word, 1980), 64.

with the children on the bed or on the carpet. And they ought to. They should play the role of horse till their knees can take it no more. They should play the monster and give chase. Life is full of rough-and-tumble experiences.

When the children get a bit older, good fathers naturally start teaching their kids skills—usually athletic skills but sometimes more specialized ones. They teach them to hit a ball, kick a ball, and catch a ball. They tend to push their children, even in play, toward skill development. They live in a world of competition and achievement, and they pass this on with a "you can do better," in counter-balance to the reassuring, "That's great!"

The Fallout of Fatherlessness

As children approach their teen years, the father becomes the key factor in the moral decisions the teen will make. If the father is home and involved, young daughters will more likely relish his attention and tender affirmation and feel no need to get it else-where. If such things are absent, daughters are at higher risk to look for them in another man and to feel a deep need to be in a relationship with a boy—any boy. Young boys without fathers (or with absent fathers) are at higher risk to look for their manhood on the streets, where manhood is proven by way of sex, drugs, crime, and dropping out of school.[4]

The man who hits the sofa and delegates family matters to his wife will immediately sow bitterness in his wife and trouble in his children. The father who is harsh and detached, who is grumpy all the time and easily angered, will raise angry and rebellious children.

Brothers, some warnings in Scripture are gender-specific because sin affects manhood in ways that differ from woman-hood. As breadwinners, we are particularly susceptible to come home tired and frustrated and want to withdraw into the mind-less cocoon of "boob-tube-ism" or some hobby that makes no

---

[4]For a good review of the impact of fatherlessness on children, see www.fatherhood.org.

demands upon us. But we are warned, "Fathers, do not provoke your children, lest they become discouraged" (Colossians 3:21). Deny children your attention and you frustrate them. Deny them your wisdom and insight as they start exploring the world around them, and you frustrate them. Ignore them or cut them off for bothering you, and you frustrate them.

Acceptance and Achievement

Mothers are absolute love. Mothers are "the steadfast love of the LORD" (Psalm 89:1) in bodily form. They bring a sense of acceptance and affirmation to the heart as both success and failure unfold in the swirl of human decision and divine sovereignty. They too look for improvement, but they lead with acceptance.

Fathers complement this. They bring their rough-and-tumble perspective with them right from the beginning, as is evident in how they play with their children, and later on in how they push them toward achievement. They tend to demand achievement *before* giving affirmation. This may explain why most people growing up in generally healthy families have absolute confidence in their mother's love and have a profound desire to win their father's approval, to do something that makes their father proud.

Shel Silverstein wrote a children's poem about this. The poem is called *Smart*, and I have found it a source of endless delight, and a reminder to me that my kids need my ongoing instruction and affirmation.

> My Dad gave me one dollar bill
> 'Cause I'm his smartest son.
> And I swapped it for two shiny quarters
> 'Cause two is more than one!
>
> And then I took the quarters
> And traded them to Lou
> For three dimes—I guess he don't know
> That three is more than two!

Just then, along came old blind Bates
And just 'cause he can't see
He gave me four nickels for my three dimes,
And four is more than three!

And I took the nickels to Hiram Coombs
Down at the seed-feed store,
And the fool gave me five pennies for them,
And five is more than four!

And then I went and showed my dad,
And he got red in the cheeks
And closed his eyes and shook his head?
Too proud of me to speak![5]

---

[5]Shel Silverstein, "Smart," *Where The Sidewalk Ends*, 35.

The Conclusion of the Matter

When I said I would die a bachelor,
I did not think I should live till I were married."
SHAKESPEARE

A desire fulfilled is sweet to the soul.
PROVERBS 13:19

No doubt we could read Shel Silverstein's poem *Smart* as a metaphor for our own life before God, our heavenly Father. He has given us various gifts, and we have rushed forth with our own reasoning and assumptions and wasted it all away with absolute certainty that we knew best. We had it figured out. We were smarter than the average bear. I had a reminder of this when I rushed out to buy a car online and did not stop to ask about how to do it right.

But God's "steadfast love is great" (Psalm 57:10). He is forbearing and patient (Romans 2:4). "He disciplines us for our good" (Hebrews 12:10). He gives good gifts to his children (Matthew 7:11). He instructs us how to live "so as to please him" (1 Thessalonians 4:1). And he promises us that in doing things right, there is "great reward" (Psalm 19:11).

This is particularly true in matters of the heart. Consider the heart to be a dollar bill. Now what will you do with it?